Healing Contentious Relationships

Healing Contentious Relationships

Overcoming the Power of Pride and Strife

Thomas Parr

Reformation Heritage Books
Grand Rapids, Michigan

Reformation Heritage Books
2965 Leonard St. NE
Grand Rapids, MI 49525
616-977-0889
orders@heritagebooks.org
www.heritagebooks.org

Scripture taken from the New King James Version®. Copyright © 1982 by Thomas Nelson. Used by permission. All rights reserved.

Printed in the United States of America
21 22 23 24 25 26/10 9 8 7 6 5 4 3 2 1

Library of Congress Cataloging-in-Publication Data

Names: Parr, Thomas (Thomas M.), author.
Title: Healing contentious relationships : overcoming the power of pride and
    strife / Thomas Parr.
Description: Grand Rapids, Michigan : Reformation Heritage Books, [2021] |
    Includes bibliographical references.
Identifiers: LCCN 2020050220 (print) | LCCN 2020050221 (ebook) | ISBN
    9781601788313 (paperback) | ISBN 9781601788320 (epub)
Subjects: LCSH: Interpersonal relations—Religious aspects—Christianity. |
    Conflict management—Religious aspects—Christianity.
Classification: LCC BV4597.52 .P375 2021 (print) | LCC BV4597.52
    (ebook) | DDC 248.4—dc23
LC record available at https://lccn.loc.gov/2020050220
LC ebook record available at https://lccn.loc.gov/2020050221

For additional Reformed literature, request a free book list from Reformation Heritage Books at the above regular or email address.

Contents

Introduction

"By pride comes nothing but strife" (Prov. 13:10). When you think about it, this statement from Proverbs is quite dogmatic. Some people interpret it as saying that the only source of contention is pride. Others understand it as saying that pride's only product is contention. Either way, the verse links pride and strife very closely. The bottom line is that if you walk into a room and encounter bad feeling and angry words between people, ungodly pride is there. Arrogance and quarreling go hand in hand.

Do you have contention and strife in your friendships, family life, or church life? Are you willing to accept that it is because of ungodly pride? You might think it is acceptable to have contention due to differences over doctrine and practice, but this is not so. It is godly to affirm doctrinal positions and to seek to live godly lives, but it is not godly to be contentious over these things—"a servant of the Lord must not quarrel but be gentle to all" (2 Tim. 2:24). *Contention* refers to strife, quarrels, and arguments. To love it is to love sin (Prov. 17:19). There is never an excuse to be harsh or cruel with one's attitudes, words, and actions, and people who claim the right to do so are arguing for sin. It is crucial to accept these absolutistic and zero-tolerance statements about contention. To live a life of peace and joy, we must take a strong stand against strife. We must want to "serve the LORD with gladness" (Ps. 100:2). Thank God this is what He wants for us!

In 2019 I had the opportunity to support a friend by going to two court hearings. I spent a few hours sitting in courtrooms and watching several cases come before the judges while I waited for my friend's case to come up. As the hours ticked by, I noticed that many if not most of the cases involved domestic abuse or violence. As a pastor, I've known couples over the years whose marriages and families were suffering due to anger and strife in the home. Despite trying to help, I've often felt very ineffective and have found myself many times fervently wishing that people would gain peace in their lives through the power of the Spirit and the Word of God. For many years I have heard from both religious and secular sources that domestic abuse is a problem of epidemic proportions in our nation. But while I was watching couple after couple stand before the judges in those hearings, it struck me that I was seeing in a very short space of time firsthand evidence of how widespread the problem is. I wanted to distance myself from the abusive men who stood, seemingly remorseful, before skeptical judges. But I realized that people who want to avoid strife must not merely avoid bad examples but must admit their own tendency to sin, and I realized that this applied to me too. We may not have traveled down the path of strife as far as others have, but we all carry with us a sinful nature, and we all fail, to some degree, at being loving with our words (James 3:2). Every one of us must continually seek God anew for empowerment over sin. This book was written to help us do so by providing insight into a passage that deals directly with the problem of strife. Christ has wondrously provided God's church with the Word and the Spirit in order for Christians to overcome sin (Ps. 119:11; Gal. 5:16). May your study of James 4 be soul-satisfying and sin-killing!

James 4 is an exposé of the pride, covetousness, and unbelief that inevitably lead to contention. In this wonderfully helpful chapter, James diagnoses where quarreling and fighting come from, and he provides essential help for having a life of peace. What people need to gain power over sin is the Word of God in a Spirit-filled heart. Therefore, this book jumps right into engaging with the text of James to get quickly to its riches even while continually pointing the reader to the gospel. The study questions at the end of each chapter are provided in the hopes that they will assist you in further meditation on James's thoughts (Ps. 1:2), and the appendix contains a list of Scripture passages for memorization (Col. 3:16).

James's chapter is *intensely practical and experiential.* It deals with the causes of strife, the patterns of it, and the solutions to it. In a world in which so many relationships are degenerating due to strife, the chapter is a much-needed help. It is also *marvelously hopeful* because it asserts that God's gracious power in Christ is given to believers who come to Him humbly and in repentance. The chapter is also *penetrating and insightful,* for it explores various ways sinful pride manifests itself. The reader can see how the disease of pride shows itself in ways other than relational strife, which allows pride to be opposed on multiple fronts, exposed wherever its Hydra heads arise, and firmly quelled by the power of the Spirit.

CHAPTER 1

The Cause and Pattern of Strife

Where do wars and fights come from among you? Do they not come from your desires for pleasure that war in your members? You lust and do not have. You murder and covet and cannot obtain. You fight and war. Yet you do not have because you do not ask. You ask and do not receive, because you ask amiss, that you may spend it on your pleasures.

—JAMES 4:1–3

James discusses three things in these opening verses. First, what causes strife? Who is to blame for it? His answer—that strife comes from our own hearts—is obvious but has massive ramifications when it is accepted and believed. Second, he shows the pattern of strife, which helpfully reveals the telltale signs that bring it about. Knowing the pattern is helpful because it allows the Christian to identify situations that bring contention out of one's heart. Third, he answers the question of why our desires go unfulfilled, and he pinpoints problems with our prayer lives and our view of God. These verses are remarkably applicational and experiential.

The Cause of Strife

James starts his chapter by teaching us an important principle—
we must not look primarily at external causes when trying to
understand quarreling and fighting. There are indeed external
factors, but these are not the primary reasons for fighting, and
if we are to get to the bottom of what causes strife, we must
look at heart issues. As Jesus taught, it is from the heart that evil
things come (Mark 7:21–22). Warring outside of us comes from
warring desires within us (James 4:1).

If a married couple is fighting a lot, for example, it is very
easy to think that the strife is happening because there is not
enough money, or she is not submissive enough, or he is too
controlling. Couples often focus on such circumstantial causes
as the main reasons for the strife in their marriages. But James
says we must look deeper; we must look at the heart.

"Where do wars and fights come from among you? Do
they not come from your desires for pleasure that war in your
members?" James locates the problem in our hearts. The word
lust ("desires for pleasure") often conjures up the basest sorts of
desires in our minds, but the Greek word doesn't demand that
we think in terms of illicit sexual desire. The word can simply mean *desire*. James is saying that quarreling comes from our
desires, our wants. Ultimately, we fight because we want things.

Recognizing that strife comes from desire ties our sinful
quarreling back to ourselves rather than our circumstances. It
blames us, not things around us. When we admit, "Yes, I yelled
because I wanted something, and I was afraid I wasn't going to
get it," we expose our sin for the base, lowly thing that it really
is, and we see ourselves as the cause of it. We're not pointing

fingers at others anymore but at ourselves. We're saying, "I am at fault. This sin came out of my own heart."

Quarrels come from us. We fight because we let something we want become so important that we are willing to sin over it. In other words, we pridefully exalt our desires over God's law. Admitting this means that we are confessing our sin (1 John 1:9). To receive forgiveness, we must not blame other people, things, or circumstances. We need to own our sin. We need to admit that we are the cause of it.

People have all sorts of justifications for why they cause strife in relationships or in the church. "He doesn't enjoy the same things as he used to." "He doesn't talk anymore." "She is always complaining." "She is never satisfied." "The church seems lifeless." Many of these external factors can be (and are) genuine problems. But how we respond to the problems is what is at issue. When a wife wants her husband to talk with her so much that she resorts to insulting him when he doesn't do so, she has caused strife because of her desires. She might claim that it's his silent treatment that is the problem, but that is avoiding her own heart issue. He may need to restart communication, but the bottom line is that the wife indulged in abusive speech because she wants him to talk. On that occasion, her desires caused strife. A husband who yells at his wife because she expresses discontent needs to recognize the same thing. Yes, she should be content, but it is his desire for peace that caused him to use abusive speech. Blaming her for provoking him ignores the heart issue of his own sin. He yelled for the simple reason that he wanted something and wasn't getting it. There's something very infantile about the root causes of sin— we sin because we want things.

The same pattern happens in church life. A church member may look at the lack of evangelistic zeal in the church and begin complaining to others in a very uncompassionate way, grumbling about "hypocrites in the church," assuming a position of spiritual superiority over the "sad sacks in the pews," and spreading contention. Does the church lack something in the area of evangelism? Certainly it does. But such critics aren't helping the situation by using the problem as an opportunity to be demeaning. The fact of the matter is that this situation is similar to the first two. The person who is causing strife wants to see others evangelize, and that desire has caused him to use abusive speech. James is right—we quarrel because we want things. The things we want might be good, but our wrong reactions when we do not get them show a heart that is committed to self rather than to God.

All sins can be boiled down to pride, covetousness, and unbelief. These master sins are three facets of the same dark gem, and James focuses on covetousness, which is simply wanting something so much that you are willing to sin against God for it. Such excessive desire is by nature faithless because it doesn't trust God as the provider of the things we want. And such desire is also self-exalting because it puts self before God. We cause strife because we pridefully exalt our own desires and do not trust God for them.

The right response to James's point is simply to accept the fact of the matter. We must look at our hearts when we try to place blame for strife. We are at fault when we speak and act in harsh, unkind ways. We wanted something and chose to fight about it. The blame is on us. As the Puritan Thomas Manton said quite bluntly, we carry an enemy in our own hearts who defaces the beauty of the soul, disturbs its order, and enslaves its will.[1] We must accept responsibility; we cause strife because of our inward desires that war within us. We must accept James's point and simply point the finger at ourselves. "You are the man!" (2 Sam. 12:7).

The Pattern of Strife

Now that James has shown us that the problem is undoubtedly with us, he proceeds to make the threefold pattern of strife quite clear. It is important to pick up on patterns because it helps us to be alert to situations in which we might be tempted. The threefold pattern is simple: We desire, we do not receive what we desire, and therefore we cause strife (James 4:2). If we received what we wanted all the time, we would not fight. It is when desires go unfulfilled that the idolatrous heart of man rises up in protest, resorting to abusive speech and causing contention. The moment we feel disappointment at unfulfilled desires, we must be on our guard, for conditions are favorable for temptation. Picking up on the pattern allows us to "feel it in our bones" when those conditions are favorable. Thus, we can be on our guard. It is like knowing rain is coming when the sky darkens with clouds.

James uses colorful language to describe this pattern. He says that not receiving what you desire causes you to murder. That's extreme language to say the least, and you might dismiss the idea on the face of it, since thankfully you've never killed anyone. But James is alluding to Jesus's words in the Sermon

---

1. Adapted from Thomas Manton, *James* (1693; repr., Edinburgh: Banner of Truth, 1988), 327.

on the Mount, in which He linked sinful anger to murder (Matt. 5:21–22). He says that anger leads to murder, and those who indulge in it are liable to eternal judgment. It is not that anger is just as sinful as murder; that would be an unbalanced conclusion, and neither Jesus nor James taught this. But sinful anger is terrible and will receive God's judgment; it needs to be exposed and forsaken. In order to highlight its evil, James links our anger to the extremity to which anger can lead. We need to sense anger as a hateful thing and a step toward heinous evil. We should sense it as the serious danger that it is. When tempted to be angry, we should feel as if we're about to step on a venomous snake.

The pattern is clear—when we desire something but do not obtain it, we become angry and cause strife. James's teaching here is so blunt that we might miss its implications. The pattern shows us something we noted earlier but in an even starker way. We cause strife due to our covetousness and overweening pride, but people who cause strife often blame the wrong thing. They won't own their sin; instead, they blame the circumstance that brought out their wrong words and behavior. How many times have you heard someone say, "Yeah, but he provoked me!" or "She cause me to stumble into sin!" It may be true that there was stumbling and provocation, but when people sin they simply need to own up to their pride and covetousness rather than focus on circumstances outside themselves.

It is crucial to see the difference between circumstantial and efficient causes. The efficient cause of an action is the real cause of it; a circumstantial cause just provides the setting in which the efficient cause manifests itself. The Puritan Thomas Goodwin used an illustration that is a bit earthy but quite helpful.

He said that a dung heap smells worse when the sun rises and heats it up. What is the cause of the worse smell? The sun's rising is indeed a cause, but it is not the efficient cause, only the circumstantial cause. The efficient cause of the worse smell (you might say the culpable cause of it) is the material in the heap. The sun was merely the circumstance that brought it out; the sun cannot be held to blame for the smell. The stink is in the heap, and so is the blame for it. It is foolish to raise your fist to the sun as if it were culpable for the heap's stench. The problem is not in the sun but in the heap.[2]

When we sin we often try to blame the circumstantial cause. We blame the thing that brought out our sin while we ignore the real cause of it—our pride, covetousness, and unbelief. We raise our fist at the circumstances that made conditions favorable for sin when actually the stink is in the heap. Yes, circumstances were conducive for sin, but circumstances don't commit evil. We're to blame for our sin. I am to blame for mine. You are to blame for yours.

Consider the case of a church librarian who stirs up strife without really being aware of her sin. She has a good desire; she wants to promote reading, so she carefully selects books to add to the church library. The selection of books starts growing nicely. But despite all her efforts, very few people check out books. Few people even visit the library room. The librarian begins voicing derogatory thoughts about people and complaining bitterly. Someone confronts her about her sinful words, and she blames the nonreading people; but their reading problems

---

2. See Thomas Goodwin, *The Works of Thomas Goodwin* (Edinburgh: James Nichol, 1865), 10:60.

are the circumstantial cause of her cruel speech. The culpable cause for her sin is herself, and for her to mention the nonreaders is to shift blame. Yes, they should read, but their lack of interest is not the culpable cause for the librarian's harsh words.

It may be difficult to relate to a story about an irritated librarian. But notice the James 4 pattern in the case, a pattern that we undoubtedly share. She wanted something that happened to be good. But when circumstances didn't turn out to fulfill her good desire, she spoke words that were hurtful and insulting. Her unfulfilled desires led to derogatory speech that stirred up contention. She quarreled because she wanted something and didn't get it. She might defend herself and say, "Well, I was provoked by these ignoramuses in the church," but that uses insulting language to blame the circumstantial cause. Her sin was caused by her ungodly response to her unfulfilled desire. Can you see yourself in this?

Consider the case of a homeschool family. The oldest child is getting serious about school, and the parents are happy to see it. But along with the child's newfound ambitions comes a whole new passel of problems. The younger children in the home are still just as rambunctious as ever. The oldest is sitting in his room trying to study algebra while the other children are making a ruckus for the tenth time in an hour. The oldest child desires quiet study, but his younger siblings aren't giving him what he wants. His anger is riled up and he breaks out in unkind words. He desires something good, but his idolatry is exposed when it is revealed he wants quiet more than he wants kindness. Yes, the smaller children should be quiet. Yes, the parents should create an environment that is conducive to academic pursuits. But circumstances aren't the direct cause of the oldest child's sin. He is speaking hard words because he isn't getting what he wants. Yet it is so easy to blame the circumstances that brought the sin rather than the heart that really caused it and is guilty for it.

Sometimes God allows us to be placed in trying circumstances so that we can see our pride and idolatry. We must not blame God or the circumstances when we fail. The circumstances simply bring out our idolatry and our commitment to self. Our hearts are the direct cause of our sin. If our hearts weren't bad, we would not be so tempted by trying circumstances. It is actually crucial to our spiritual health to simply look at ourselves and let the blame for our sin fall there. If we make excuses and point fingers, we avoid the conviction that drives us to Christ. We must let our failure in trying circumstances reveal our heart so that we cry out to God for grace and so the Spirit will transform us more into the image of Christ.

Recognize that your bad behavior stems from your bad heart. This is the fundamental place from which James launches his discussion of healing relational strife. It is where we need to start if we want to heal relationships. Own your sin and the sinful heart that produces it. Do not shift responsibility or blame others, but say with the publican, "God, be merciful to me a sinner" (Luke 18:13). The publican's language is actually "me, *the* sinner." It is the verbal equivalent of a pointed finger, but he is pointing it at himself and not blaming his circumstances or other people. This is in contrast to the Pharisee who compares himself (favorably) with others (Luke 18:11).

Let's be clear about the pattern that leads to strife. We want things, often good things, but when in God's good providence we do not get what we want, we are tempted to desire those things more than we want joy in Christ and sweet obedience to Him. If our heart is more committed to self than to God, strife will result as we protest and wrangle to try to gain our desires.

Why Our Desires Go Unfulfilled

"Yes, OK, I sinned. I should not have become angry when my desire was unmet. I admit I was idolatrous, but boy was I in a hard circumstance! I mean, the Bible even says that 'hope deferred makes the heart sick.' Can't you have a little compassion? How would you fare if you were put into such hot water?"

This might be a response of someone who recognizes his sin but also sees how painful and disappointing unfulfilled desires can be, how hard circumstances can become. Responses like this show willingness to admit sin, but they also make a point: it is normal to desire things and to be extremely disappointed when our desires go unfulfilled. I think we can all relate to the objection, "C'mon, have a little compassion!" It is a point well taken, though not an excuse for sin.

It is undoubtedly true that "hope deferred makes the heart sick" (Prov. 13:12). Unmet desires can be and often are painful. Of course, there is no excuse for abusive speech and contention. No unfulfilled desire justifies cruelty, angry outbursts, or insults. If we sin in these ways, we must simply own our sin (and our sinful hearts) and seek forgiveness and empowerment in the gospel of Jesus Christ. This is what James wants us to do when we fall into causing strife.

But James also addresses how to deal with the unfulfilled desires themselves: "You do not have because you do not ask. You ask and do not receive, because you ask amiss, that you may spend it on your pleasures" (James 4:2–3). In this statement there is a marvelous underlying presupposition—a view of God as generous and wanting to give that is mirrored in many other texts of Scripture. God wants to fill you with good things (Ps. 103:5). He richly gives you all things to enjoy (1 Tim. 6:17). He wants you to experience goodness and mercy all your days (Ps. 23:6). God is generous and wants to delight our hearts. Of course, this is not a prosperity gospel that denies there will be suffering in this life (Mark 10:30; John 16:33). But James is identifying why our desires go unfulfilled (which he says is a problem with our prayers), and therefore he is clearly encouraging believers to seek God for their desires: "You do not have because you do not ask" (James 4:2).

After making the initial point that strife comes from us and that we ought to own the sins we cause, it is surprising that James does not keep convicting us or immediately give us solutions to strife. Instead he assures us that God wants to fulfill our (good) desires, even ones that we cause strife over. That is remarkable; he offers gospel before bringing law. He wants us to realize that God is caring and openhanded. He's telling us that the lack we experience is not ideal and that we ought to pray to God about it. We shouldn't sin because of unfulfilled desires, but God does want us to address these by seeking everything from His kind heart. Believing the good news that God is generous and large-hearted is fundamental to relaxing and trusting Him and praying to Him, not to mention being a peacemaker with others.

James tells us two things about how to deal with unfulfilled desires. We must first seek our desires from God Himself, through prayer. Second, we must seek our desires with pure motives, putting God first. If we fail in these two things, we sin against God. We exclude God as provider, which is a sign we don't trust Him; and wanting things just to consume on our own lusts shows that we do not acknowledge Him as chief good in our lives. Living independently from God (faithlessness) and loving pleasure more than we love Him (covetousness) are two fatal errors. James is helping us see how to seek joy in this world hand in hand with God. He is showing us how to avoid turning everything we want into an idol that we'll wrangle and create strife over; he's showing us how to honor God as we roam His good earth delighting in His good things. Nothing is easier for fallen people than to love the gifts but ignore the giver. Let's look closer at James's two points about how to deal with our unfulfilled desires.

First, we must seek fulfillment of our desires from God Himself, not independently from Him. "You do not have because you do not ask" (James 4:2). He's talking about living by faith, asking God to meet the need you feel so poignantly; he's talking about prayer and how our painful lack comes from our prayerlessness. God is generous, ready to provide for our real needs and legitimate desires, but He wants to be entreated for them (Matt. 7:7). God wants us to come to Him as our provider and to seek everything at His hand. In fact, God makes prayer necessary; if prayer is lacking, God's supply stops.

Earlier in the book, James said that God is the Father of lights, from whom every good and perfect gift comes (James 1:17). The objective reality is that everything we have comes from the generous God who constantly showers us with goodness. But God wants us to acknowledge this reality by actively seeking Him for everything. Doing so is to subjectively live according to the objective reality of who God is as the fountain of every blessing. It is a practical confession of faith in God as the living God, the One with whom we have to do, the provider and preserver of all things. James is saying that if you ask, you will have, because God loves to hear His children pray and loves to provide for their needs. God is generous, so we should come to Him as the generous giver He is. Doing so honors God as He has revealed Himself to be.

Yet we do not have because we do not come and seek all things from Him. John Calvin, echoing James, shows how crucial it is to have the right view of God as magnanimous and big-hearted, not stingy:

> It will not suffice simply to hold that there is One whom all ought to honor and adore, unless we are also persuaded that he is the fountain of every good, and that we must seek nothing elsewhere than in him…. Until men recognize that they owe everything to God, that they are nourished by his fatherly care, that he is the Author of their every good, that they should seek nothing beyond him—they will never yield him willing service.[3]

Second, James tells us that we must pray with a pure heart: "You ask and do not receive, because you ask amiss, that you may spend it on your pleasures" (James 4:3). He seems to be ready to answer an objection, such as, "Yes, I did pray, but God didn't provide for my need." Aside from the fact that God sometimes tells us to wait, James is saying that sometimes we want things and even pray for them without the glory of God or the good of His people in mind; rather, we are focusing only

---

3. John Calvin, *Institutes of the Christian Religion*, ed. John T. McNeill, trans. Ford Lewis Battles (Philadelphia: Westminster Press, 1960), 1.2.1.

or primarily on ourselves and our own desires. In other words, we don't receive what we want because our motives are not pure. We must repent and come to God with a pure heart, with our priorities straight and our motives committed to honoring God first and foremost.

There is a reason that our prayers must be properly motivated if they are to receive a positive answer—God is greatest and most glorious and therefore must be first in our lives. The first question of the Westminster Shorter Catechism asks, "What is the chief end of man?" It answers, "Man's chief end is to glorify God, and to enjoy him forever." Paul says we should make it our goal to glorify God in all our actions (1 Cor. 10:31) and that God created everything for His own pleasure and honor and glory: "All things were created through Him and for Him" (Col. 1:16). Once again, there is an objective, theological reality we must subjectively reflect in our experience. The objective reality is that God made us primarily for His glory, honor, and pleasure. Seeking God primarily for ourselves subverts that. It puts self above God and is fundamentally idolatrous. Putting God first, in His rightful place, is what getting our priorities straight means. Unless we can be sure we are putting God first, how can we know we are serving God at all?

When we pray just so we can get what we want, we must know God doesn't listen to the idolatrous. He doesn't coddle the selfish. He doesn't encourage narcissism. He doesn't feed our fallen natures. He made us for Himself; we must not live for ourselves. Our sinful natures subvert the God-honoring purpose for our existence and seek to place ourselves in God's rightful place. He will not relate with those who are so diametrically opposed to His purposes. "If I regard iniquity in my heart, the Lord will not hear" (Ps. 66:18). As Calvin put it, we must not attempt to "make God the minister of [our] own lusts."[4] Perhaps you need to fall down on your face before God and confess your self-centered lifestyle, pleading with Him to renew a right spirit within you (Ps. 51:10). It is a wondrous testimony to God's grace that He receives repentant sinners who flee to Christ humbly and broken over their sin.

Ask yourself some questions: "Do I really believe God is generous?" "Do I seek Him to have my needs met, or do I have an independent attitude?" "Do I want what I want primarily for myself, or is the orientation of my life one that seeks the glory of God first, so that my desires are primarily about God and promoting His interests?"

In short, James says that our lack, the lack over which we can cause strife, comes from two things: (1) a lack of faith in the generous God, which leads us to fail to seek all things from His hand, and (2) a covetousness that leads us to make even our prayer life about ourselves. Again, this boils down to pride, covetousness, and unbelief. The same things that cause us to mistreat people cause us to mistreat God in prayer. It is of course wrong to say that every unanswered prayer is the result of sin on the part of the one praying, and James isn't making that claim. After all, God does tell us to wait, but James is correct to pinpoint our fallen natures and their tendency to exalt self over God.

One of the most beautiful things about these two points is to consider them in their context. Instead of going after us

---

4. John Calvin, *Calvin's Commentaries*, vol. 22, *Commentaries on the Epistle of James* (Grand Rapids: Baker, 1999), 330.

solely to rebuke us and bring us under conviction of sin, James presents a view of God as generous, giving, and large-hearted, wanting to give but holding back because of our unbelief and base greed. Yet by putting these verses here, God shows us the way to blessing and satisfied desires. Ultimately James is implying that God wants us to be happy! But not at the expense of godliness. To top it off, the marvelous thing about Christ's salvation is that both godliness and eternal happiness are ideals that will be fully realized in heaven. Man's sin, my sin, your sin, will not defeat God's purpose of everlasting joy.

Study Questions

1. If we are to get to the bottom of the cause of strife, we must look at _____ issues. How does Mark 7:21–22 teach this idea?

2. How are pride, covetousness, and unbelief related as causes of sin?

3. Can our desires for *good* things end up being causes of sin? How can this be?

4. We fight because we let something we _____ become so important that we are willing to _____ because of it.

5. What desires do you have that you might be tempted to create strife over?

6. What is the threefold pattern of strife?

7. What is the difference between a circumstantial cause and an efficient cause? How does Thomas Goodwin illustrate the difference?

8. What is the similarity between the irritated librarian and the oldest child in the homeschool family?

9. Can you think of a time when you blamed circumstances for your sinful response to them?

10. How should we respond when we fail in trying circumstances? How does Luke 18:13 help us see how to respond?

11. What is James's underlying assumption about God when he says we do not have because we do not ask? See 1 Timothy 6:17 and Psalm 103:5.

12. Why should we seek everything from God's hand rather than independently of Him? List as many reasons as you can find in the chapter.

13. Why is the Westminster Shorter Catechism's first question so important? What Bible verses can you find that support the catechism's statement?

CHAPTER 2

Confronted as Sinners

Adulterers and adulteresses! Do you not know that friendship with the world is enmity with God? Whoever therefore wants to be a friend of the world makes himself an enemy of God. Or do you think that the Scripture says in vain, "The Spirit who dwells in us yearns jealously"?

—JAMES 4:4–5

Let's sum up what James has explained so far about healing relational strife. He's told us that strife is caused when we pridefully exalt our desires, and therefore we shouldn't blame others or our circumstances for our sin. We should admit that we are to blame for contributing to quarrels. We should admit that, when our desires go unfulfilled, we protest and verbally mistreat those whom we perceive as contributing to our pain. Rather than pray, we quarrel. And when we do pray, we pray self-centeredly, wanting our desires to be met for our own pleasure. So even our prayers become expressions of an ungodly, idolatrous heart.

James has done quite a good job of exposing the corruptions of our fallen nature! The display of our fleshly commitment to self, and our willingness to exalt self over God, ought to humble us greatly. James wants us to be humbled by it too, so he begins confronting us quite bluntly about our sinfulness.

Adulterers!

James uses the shocking label *adulterer* to get us to wake up to the depth of our problem. He wants us to experience real healing, so we must see the problem for what it is. If we don't, we won't treat it the way it needs to be treated. We must not place a bandage on our bone cancer. We must not minimize our problem but face it in all of its seriousness. We also cannot avoid the problem by saying to ourselves, "How can I change so I can start getting answers to my prayers and get what I want?" James knows that such a motive is still rooted in the selfishness that causes strife to begin with. True healing demands that we face up to our true spiritual condition—we are unfaithful to God. And so James exposes the corruption and deep-seated commitment to self that is causing all the problems. He is not engaged in name-calling; he is accurately diagnosing the problem without sugarcoating anything. But he is addressing us in a very shocking way: "You adulterers!"

An adulterer is a covenant breaker. More than that, an adulterer is unfaithful to a marriage covenant, a bond that the vast majority of people even in our corrupt times see as precious. Many people even today would see it as a tragedy to destroy a marriage through infidelity. But that is what infidelity does. It breaks the covenant. In a marriage covenant, one of the key stipulations is remaining sexually faithful to the one partner. A husband must forsake all others and be faithful in body and soul to his spouse. The same goes for a wife. Adultery is the sin of breaking this vow, and it breaks the covenant.

Of course, James is talking about spiritual rather than physical adultery. He says that people whose relationships have devolved into contention and who pray so they can get things to consume on their lusts are spiritual adulterers. James is continuing the grand Old Testament tradition of comparing the people's relationship with God to a marriage (e.g., Hos. 3:1). Capitulating to sin is wickedness and evil, and it is unfaithfulness to God.

When we cause strife, our main problem is not the relational friction we are causing with others. The main problem is that our sin is against God. That is where we should focus our attention. When we see that we are causing relational strife and are focused primarily on our own desires, we must recognize we are not right with God, and we must heal our relationship with Him, first and foremost. Recognizing this brings our relationship with God to the forefront of our minds, just as it should be.

But there are several reasons why Christians might avoid letting James confront them. They might simply be hard-hearted. Sometimes conservative Christian people can almost begin to feel that they are no longer sinners. I've heard it before: "Pastor, stop telling me to get things right. Me and God, we're OK." Many Christian people have gone to church and been part of Christian circles for so long that they simply don't feel guilty or unworthy anymore. A smug, self-congratulatory state of mind creeps over them. They first came to Christ admitting their sin, but it has been a long time since they felt sinful. They would never say they've achieved sinless perfection—thankfully they're too doctrinally correct for that. But they don't feel wretched or humbled before God. Unlike Paul, who referred to himself later in life as the chief of sinners (1 Tim. 1:15), their "sanctification" has made them less sensible of their sin. It is important to recognize that godly people grow in power over sin, but they never grow insensible of it. In fact, they grow more sensible of it.

Christians might think that Reformed doctrine justifies a lethargic view of the Christian life. Enjoying God's sovereign grace does not eliminate the need to wage continual warfare against sin. The Westminster Confession of Faith, in describing sanctification, states that there abides "still some remnants of corruption in every part; whence ariseth a continual and irreconcilable war" (WCF 13.2). The Christian life isn't a playground; it is a battleground. Spiritual maturity does not mean never having to get right with God and topple over idols anymore. A true grasp of Reformed doctrine leads one to be always reforming—*semper reformanda*. True Christianity is a lifestyle of repentance, for as long as we are in this world, we carry the flesh around with us. Yes, we should grow in grace, and true Christians experience dramatic and substantial growth, thank God. But we should never feel that we no longer need to fight sin. J. C. Ryle said that "the believer may be known by his inward warfare as well as by his inward peace."[1] Feeling no need to fight against sin is a sign of capitulation rather than victory, of ungodliness rather than godliness. God forbid that we should hear James saying to us, "You adulterers!" and think "He must be talking to someone else; that couldn't be me." Let his rebuke land on your conscience. Let him accost you and take you by the shoulders, as it were, and confront you. Let his warning cause you to search yourself deeply and honestly. Let it

---

1. J. C. Ryle, *Expository Thoughts on John* (1869; repr., Edinburgh: Banner of Truth, 1999), 2:389.

create in you a great watchfulness over your own soul, and let it cause you to flee earnestly to Christ for help in the fight against your sin, for Christ alone is the strong tower where we are safe.

Christians also might think that accepting the label of "spiritual adulterer" threatens key doctrines. If we admit that the label of spiritual adulterers either can or actually does apply to us, it raises the question, How severe is our condition? If being an adulterer means being a covenant breaker, have we then destroyed our covenant with God? Is it possible to do so? Someone might feel that to accept the label would mean denying the perseverance of the saints or that they have lost their salvation. But this is not the case. True believers always persevere to the end and never perish (John 10:28–30). Though we sin, and though each sin truly is an instance of unfaithfulness to God, He has promised in the covenant of grace to give us Christ's perfect righteousness as our own (1 Cor. 1:30). And He has provided Christ's effective cross-work to pay the penalty for all our sin—He canceled "the record of debt that stood against us" (Col. 2:14 ESV). The power of Christ's righteous life, bitter death, and glorious resurrection cannot be defeated by our sinfulness. Furthermore, God has promised us not only saving grace in Christ but also empowering grace through the Holy Spirit (Gal. 5:16). Therefore, we can trust that His covenant of grace will even provide empowerment for our practical obedience. Our fruit is from Him (Hos. 14:8). Believers have Christ's imputed righteousness, the cleansing of Christ's effective atonement, and the empowerment of Christ's Holy Spirit. In so many wonderful ways, God has supplied all our needs in Christ. Nevertheless, when we sin, we must confess that we have been unfaithful to God. We confess this not to be saved again (for it is impossible to lose one's salvation, let alone to try to regain it) but to reconsecrate our lives to Him. We must renew our commitment to the covenant that He made with us. We are prone to wander, and we must get back on the narrow way when we step off it. Thankfully, for those in God's family by faith in the cross, we can be assured that nothing can separate us from the love of God in Christ Jesus our Lord, not even our unfaithfulness.

In short, James says that if we are causing relational strife, we must evaluate ourselves accurately and honestly. We must admit that we are spiritual adulterers and have been unfaithful to God. It is not a denial of important doctrine to admit our sinfulness and continuing struggles. In fact, it is crucial to do so. We must maintain a sense of our frailty, weakness, and our sin; if we do, it will encourage us to have constant recourse to the Savior, who "ever lives to intercede for us" and who alone is the answer to all our needs.

Friends of the World and Enemies of God

James now begins defending his use of the term *adulterers*, which might be quite a pill to swallow. He says that our sinful words and behavior show that we are friends of the world, and anyone who is a friend of the world is in a state of antagonism toward God (James 4:4). He repeats this idea twice, once as a rhetorical question and once as a direct assertion, and thus the Holy Spirit chose to emphasize it quite strongly in this letter, which we must remember was written to believers (1:16; 2:1). James wants us to know that he was entirely justified in using the term *adulterer* in addressing the covenant community. If we are committed to self in our prayers and if we are creating strife over unfulfilled desires, we have become unfaithful to the all-sufficient God. Therefore, James couldn't have chosen a better term than *adulterer*. We profess to enjoy God's covenantal love but now have turned from Him. I'm inclined to say that this is treachery, and such an extreme word may not be overstating it. Whatever word we use to describe it, our unfaithfulness ought to bring us to tears of regret and repentance.

James wants to fix our spiritual eye on what we've done to God. James knows that all our sin is primarily against God (Ps. 51:4). He knows that we are naturally quite blind to how our sins reflect poorly on God and cast aspersions on His glory. And he knows that if we get right with God, our sins in our other relationships will begin to heal.

Something within us may object to being told that we are spiritual adulterers against God, so if we are to submit to the apostle's teaching—and to the Holy Spirit who inspired his words—we must allow James to argue for it. Let's consider two points on how he defends his calling us adulterers.

First, James tells us that our strife shows that we have fallen into the sin of being friends of the world. There is a sense in which it is right to be a friend of the world. "God so loved the world," and we are grateful that Jesus is a friend of sinners. Like Him, we too must care about sinners and desire their salvation and blessing. It would be arrogant and evil to think of ourselves as superior to other sinners, much as the Pharisee did in Luke 18:9–14. When James says that it is wrong to be a friend of the world, he is not saying that we should walk around with our noses in the air as if we're better than others.

But the Bible often uses the term *world* not to refer to people in general but to fallen humanity as postured against God and in antagonism to Him. Jesus showed this use of the term when He prayed to the Father, "I do not pray for the world but for those whom You have given Me, for they are Yours" (John 17:9). The word *world* refers to humanity as they carry out their evil philosophies, habits, ways, and deeds. The apostle John tells us, "Do not love the world or the things in the world. If anyone loves the world, the love of the Father is not in him. For all that is in the world—the lust of the flesh, the lust of the eyes, and the pride of life—is not of the Father but is of the world" (1 John 2:15–16). Though we can be the friend of sinners, we cannot accommodate their worldview. We must not be friends with the world in this sense, as sharing in its evil thoughts and ways.

James is saying that causing relational strife and praying with our lusts as most important are clearly examples of friendship with the world in its evil. These sins certainly do not honor God. They do not put Him first, as we must do, since He is the most glorious and inherently valuable person in existence. Jesus tells us that in comparison to our love for Him, our love for our closest loved ones must be hate (Luke 14:26). His words on this point are shocking, but of course He is right; we must value most what is most valuable. To do otherwise is an error in judgment, but it is far worse than that, for it is an affront to God and exalts the creation over the creator. We must prioritize loving the Lord our God with all our heart, soul, mind, and strength (Mark 12:30). Failing to do so is clearly equivalent to aligning ourselves with the world, which lies in the power of the wicked one (1 John 5:19). To use cruel words and create strife is to reject God's commands against strife (e.g., Phil. 2:1–4) and to step onto the side of the world. To pray to God just to consume things on our lusts is to want to enlist God in our self-ish agenda. We have subsumed God's interests beneath our own. We have become friends of the world, and this friendship shows our unfaithfulness to God.

Second, James says that our friendship with the world is equivalent to "enmity with" or hatred for God. How is this the case? Loving God first is the great obligation of being in covenant with Him; therefore, aligning oneself with the world, which rejects God, is clearly to take a posture of hatred against Him. You might be skeptical and think, "But I don't have hate feelings in my heart against God! I love God." Nevertheless, if loving God means keeping His commandments, then disobedience is to hate Him. To bring this principle to the matter at hand, to cause strife and contention is to commit an act of hostility toward God. Perhaps there are many people who think and speak of themselves as loving God, but their actions contradict their words. God cares deeply about our behavior, and it is very easy to choose things and think things and feel things that are hostile to Him. It is very easy for us to "hate" God and offend Him.

You might object to all of this on the basis of how sensitive life becomes if you were to accept what James is saying. "I'd have to watch everything I do! There are a million and one ways to go astray! Endless ways to offend God, to 'hate' Him! This can't be how God wants me to live my life—such precision, such scruples, such painstaking care being taken over everything in life!" Exactly. This is why people object. This is why people justify sin. It is why people keep harming their relationships and remain in chains of lust. They resist viewing things the exacting way God sees them, because they think life will be unbearable if they do, and they'd rather have the evil status quo than become serious about godliness. They can't see that viewing God as holy and offended at sin allows them a precious opportunity to repent and confess and to experience God's matchless grace in the gospel. Being sensitive about the many ways we stray allows us to really see how generous God is in the cross. Seeing God as holy is the first step in truly melting before His mercy. By avoiding conviction, and wanting freedom to do what we want without guilt, we have robbed ourselves of joy in Christ. How important it is that we allow our failure to obey to show us our guilt so that we will turn our eyes on Christ to see His perfect righteousness.

The Puritan Richard Rogers (1551–1618) was one of the first to attempt to describe the Puritan lifestyle. He was known for taking the Christian life very seriously, and he sought to put God first with all of his heart, but this lifestyle, which some might call severe, often led him to lament his failings and weaknesses. Yet he took comfort in the gospel. Once, when a friend told him that he was too precise, he replied, "I serve a precise God." How true! This is exactly how James portrays God. He is exacting about what is right and wrong. God is holy. To commit the sin of strife is to be spiritually unfaithful and show hostility to Him.

Recognizing your enmity to God is crucial for getting right with Him. If you have fallen into sin and are justifying it, perpetuating it, excusing it, even praying for it, you must confess your friendship with the world and hatred for God. You must confess your spiritual adultery. There is nothing better for you than to flee to God in repentance. Fall on your face before God in dismay at your terrible sin against your loving Lord. Run to the grace of God found in Jesus Christ, finding joy all over again in His amazing love that would descend even to a wretch like you. You are not being saved again; it is not possible to be saved and lost, because believers in Christ cannot lose their salvation (John 10:28). But the experience of renewing one's covenant after a time of going astray can feel quite similar to conversion. If you have caused relational strife, you should flee to Christ in repentance and experience anew the amazing grace of God, who in His vast mercy sticks closer than a brother to people like us. Stand in awe that He didn't leave you when you were insensible to your wretched state. Stare in wonder with the eye of faith at our holy Lord who saves, sanctifies, and promises to glorify sinners like us. Only those who feel their sin will marvel at God's grace toward sinners. And marveling at grace in Christ will empower you to hate the very thought of causing strife.

"Lusting to Envy" or "Yearning Zealously"

There is some debate over what James means when he says "The Spirit who dwells in us yearns jealously" (James 4:5). He might be referring to our fallen nature's desire to go against God and His ways, similar to the description of the heathen raging and bursting God's bonds (Ps. 2:1–3). In which case the idea is "our human spirit that dwells in us lusts enviously against God." Or James might mean that God desires to have our love and loyalty: "God's Spirit who dwells in us yearns zealously over us." Both interpretations promote biblical truths. God desires all of our hearts, and in our fallen natures we desire to go against God. In a fallen world, both ideas presume each other. God reaches out to man, but man runs away from God.

Rather than choose an interpretation, let's consider both of these biblical truths, because both fit quite well in the flow of James's argument. He has been saying that our causing strife is evidence of spiritual unfaithfulness against God. Now he goes on to explain either that our unfaithfulness goes against God's yearning for us or that it fits with what we already know about our corrupt nature yearning for sin. Therefore, we will explore God's yearning for us, then our corrupt natures.

First, God yearns for all of our hearts, and He isn't content with half-hearted devotion (Rev. 3:16). Jesus said our love for our closest loved ones should be like hate in comparison with our love for Him (Luke 14:26). Of course this doesn't mean that we should hate our loved ones—Jesus is speaking comparatively. It means that we should recognize the priority of loving God. The first commandment is to love God with all our heart, mind, soul, and strength. God deserves our greatest love and loyalty. Someone once said that God wants all our loyalty, while the devil is content with just a little; if he can succeed in dividing our heart, that means God doesn't have all of it.

That God deserves our utmost devotion is self-evident to people who have the Spirit; they know it instinctively and don't have to be taught that God is their Lord to whom they have sworn homage and fealty and who has ultimate claim to their lives. He alone is worthy, deserving of our complete devotion, and this is, in a very basic sense, what it means for God to be God. But even if it is instinctive to believers, it also makes logical sense and can be explained quite cogently. God deserves all of our hearts for several reasons.

God deserves our devotion because He created us. The creator naturally has ownership rights over His creation. In human relations and laws we understand this, for example, in the concept of intellectual property. If a person comes up with an idea, that idea is theirs, and they deserve credit and any remuneration the idea is seen to merit. The entire universe is God's intellectual property, so to speak, for He spoke and all things came to be (Ps. 33:6, 9). This gives God an ownership and a right over all things that must be acknowledged. To deny Him this right is unjust; it's a revolt against what is equitable, an attempted theft of what is rightfully His. All things were created "for Him" (Col. 1:16). Therefore, God deserves reverence for being the rightful Master and Owner of all things. We should not live as though we have no creator to whom we should give honor; we should glorify Him as our benevolent master.

God also deserves our devotion because He has given us every good thing we've ever enjoyed. He is not sitting stingily over creation, hoarding blessings to Himself. God is generous by nature and wants to share what He owns with His creatures. God gives us "richly all things to enjoy" (1 Tim. 6:17). He gives to everyone "life, breath, and all things" (Acts 17:25). Everything is a gift, and no one has ever enjoyed any good thing except what God has given in His providence. People may use God's gifts wrongly, but even when misdirected they are still from Him. Our most delightful family members, friendships, and experiences are just drops from an ocean of goodness in the heart of God. They are good and delightful because He is far more good and delightful. They bear His imprint. God is like a fountain gushing cold, clear water in an ever-constant flow. The earth is full of His riches (Ps. 104:24). Therefore, we should not think of ourselves as independent and self-sufficient; we should recognize our state of dependence on God and give

Him gratitude and glory as our benevolent provider. It takes humility to do this, but it is a humility that is true to reality. To insist on self-sufficiency is to close one's eyes to the truth. It is like a small child denying that he needs his parents to feed and clothe and care for him.

God also deserves our devotion because He is by nature transcendent. This means that God transcends everything in greatness and intrinsic worth. As the psalmist puts it, "The LORD is high above all nations, His glory above the heavens. Who is like the LORD our God, who dwells on high" (Ps. 113:4–5). This idea of transcendence might seem a little difficult, but an illustration helps clear it up. If you were playing basketball with a group of average Americans and then Michael Jordan in his prime were to join your game and play his best, you would have no problem understanding the idea of transcendence. Such a player would seem so far above all the others that they simply couldn't compare with him. That is the idea in a nutshell. But as helpful as this illustration is, it can distort the truth about God, for the players are all human, even the one who is far better than the rest. God is not a man. As one theologian put it, "He is as high above an archangel as he is above a caterpillar, for the gulf that separates the archangel from the caterpillar is but finite, while the gulf between God and the archangel is infinite."[2] With God it is really true—no one can compare with Him. God is off the charts on the scale of intrinsic worth. He is so transcendent above mankind that He compares Himself to a potter and us to clay (Isa. 64:8). This

2. A. W. Tozer, *The Knowledge of the Holy* (New York: Harper & Row, 1975), 76.

means we should not try to bring God down to our level or judge Him by human standards. We should glorify Him as the high and lofty God, giving Him the honor due to Him.

God deserves our devotion because He redeemed us by Jesus Christ. Taken with the previous reasons, this is so compelling. We are clay in comparison to God, and He could have thrown away the defective clay, but He didn't. The transcendent God who created all and sustains all can do what He wants with His creation. He has total sovereign rights over it all, including over us. That places us in the position of being completely at God's mercy—a disturbing prospect when you consider the fall and our many sins. We are not only dependent on God, but we are rebels against Him. What did God do when people revolted, broke His law, and sinned against Him? Did he cast away the rebellious clay? Did He withdraw His providential control and bring His creation crashing down in fire and ruin? No, though He does plan to punish transgressors. Instead of casting it all away, He began a history of redemption, planned in eternity and beginning at Genesis 3:15, in which He promised to send a savior to defeat Satan and reverse the curse, at the cost of suffering injury Himself.

God's immense mercy in Jesus Christ is best appreciated against the backdrop of both human sin and God's rights. God was entirely within His rights to no longer providentially preserve those who revolted against Him, but instead of expelling us from creation He "demonstrates His own love toward us, in that while we were still sinners, Christ died for us" (Rom. 5:8). This fact about the transcendent God, that He is gracious and merciful to sinners such as us, ought to cause us to lift up our voices in joyful, reverent praise. Such praise is the very hymn of heaven: "Worthy is the Lamb who was slain to receive power and riches and wisdom, and strength and honor and glory and blessing!" (Rev. 5:12). God deserves our utmost honor because of His great grace in Christ.

To sum up this first point about God's yearning for all of our devotion, God does so because He deserves it. He is the greatest and most glorious One, and for Him to promote supremely loving anything other than Himself would be to promote idolatry. It is right for Him to require our obedience and demand first place in our hearts. He alone is Creator, Provider, the transcendent God, and our gracious and merciful redeemer in Christ.

Second, the other interpretation of James 4:5 is also true— our fallen natures yearn for sin instead of God. In Adam we want the biblical God the way a pickpocket wants a beat cop. The heart of man produces constant sin; his heart and mind produce only that which is evil continually (Gen. 6:5). As the Westminster Confession puts it, "We are utterly indisposed, disabled, and made opposite to all good, and wholly inclined to all evil" (WCF 6.4). In light of God's zeal for our wholehearted devotion, this news about our lack of enthusiasm (to put it mildly) is far from good.

Even after salvation, Christians still struggle with their fallen nature. The situation does vastly improve after salvation; we gain significant empowerment over sin. Paul even promises believers that "sin shall not have dominion over you" (Rom. 6:14), meaning that God will sufficiently empower believers to have a great degree of sanctification in this life, though we will not reach perfection till glorification in the next life—we deceive ourselves if we say that we have no sin at any time in this life (1 John 1:8). This promised victory over sin is won through constant struggle against our fallen nature that dogs us and clings to us. Paul tells us that our Christian life may be described as a constant battle: "The flesh lusts against the Spirit, and the Spirit against the flesh; and these are contrary to one another" (Gal. 5:17). John Flavel said that "the greatest difficulty in conversion is to win the heart to God, and the greatest difficulty after conversion is to keep the heart with God."[3] The book of Jude tells Christians that one of their chief goals ought to be to "keep yourselves in the love of God"; that is, keep yourselves loving God (Jude 21). These statements portray the Christian life as a continual struggle, and they accurately represent the truth of the matter, because there is still something within us that wants to go astray. There is a devil and a world that would love to tempt us to go astray. But they couldn't gain any traction if we didn't have the flesh. As an old proverb says, "The enemy without could not harm us but for the traitor within."

So what is James trying to accomplish by asking the rhetorical question in verse 5: "Do you think that the Scripture says in vain, 'The Spirit who dwells in us yearns jealously?'" James seems to be highlighting our sensitive position. We're in relationship with a holy God who wants and justly deserves all of our hearts, yet we are "prone to wander," as the hymn writer put it. God is so great that He deserves our total devotion, yet we can very easily ignore Him, exalt self, commit sin, and avoid giving Him honor. That's a touchy situation, to be sure, and it has massive ramifications when we recognize it. Recognizing

---

3. John Flavel, *Keeping the Heart* (1667; repr., Morgan, Pa.: Soli Deo Gloria, 1998), 1.

God's exalted rights as well as our own prideful tendency to tread on them opens our eyes to our need of continually mortifying the flesh (Rom. 8:13). We should have a holy fear and distrust of ourselves, remind ourselves often of God's rights over us, and remember that we are insensitive to His rights and so very easily flout them and neglect them. Recognizing God's rights and our bent to exalt our own should also cause us to rely on God for the filling of the Spirit to empower us and open our eyes. It ought to lead us to feel keenly our inability and to be completely dependent on God's all-sufficiency and His gracious kindness and immense patience. It also should lead us to be precise and serious about holiness since God is serious about it. Finally, we must be led to sheer joy and gratitude at God's covenant of grace. That God would enter into a covenant with His Son before the foundation of the world to send Him to save sinners and rebels like us! That Christ would humble Himself to be found in fashion as a man, in the "likeness of sinful flesh"! That He would live a righteous life for us, die a sacrificial death for us, and rise ever to live for us at the Father's right hand! Such considerations should lead us to decidedly repent of our many wanderings, rest comfortably in God's grace, and commit once again to put Him first.

Study Questions

1. What is spiritual adultery?

2. What does this statement mean in context: "We must not place a bandage on our bone cancer"?

3. When we fall into creating strife with others, we should realize we must heal our relationship with _____ first and foremost.

4. Is it spiritually healthy not to sense our sinfulness? How can we grow in power over sin yet gain a greater sense of our sin?

5. What did J. C. Ryle mean when he said, "The believer may be known by his inward warfare as well as by his inward peace"?

6. What are James's two points that defend his use of the term *adulterer*?

7. In what sense should we love the world? In what sense is it a sin to love the world?

8. How is it that being a friend of the world shows unfaithfulness and antagonism to God?

9. What precious opportunity does viewing God as holy and offended at sin provide?

10. Why does God deserve our utmost love and loyalty?

11. Why did James add this question: "Do you think that the Scripture says in vain, 'The Spirit who dwells in us yearns jealously?'"

12. How should we respond to the truth that God justly deserves our total devotion yet our corrupt natures are disinclined to give it?

CHAPTER 3

Grace to Overcome Sin and Strife

*But He gives more grace. Therefore He says: "God resists the
proud, but gives grace to the humble."*
—JAMES 4:6

James has shown us the depths of our sin and confronted us
quite directly about it. He demonstrates that we are to blame
for the strife and misery we cause—our sin comes from our
own hearts when we experience unfulfilled desires, and we cannot blame our sin on others. James has established that we don't
seek God for our unfulfilled desires as we should. And when we
do seek God, even our prayers can become self-centered mono-
logues. He has shown us that we are unfaithful to God when
He so rightfully deserves our utmost loyalty and honor. James
4:1–5 is a theological and experiential drubbing, and it should
leave us longing for an answer to our sinful natures that so easily
lead us astray into sinful strife. It is still quite true: we must feel
our sin before we can truly seek God for His grace. James has
taken away our excuses and told us that we are the problem.
Our pride, covetousness, and unbelief threaten to wreak havoc
in our relationships.

At verse 6 James begins to explain the glorious solution to the problem. Once we really accept our sinful state, our hearts naturally seek a solution. And though James (undeservedly) has a reputation for being a "legal" epistle, he clearly points to God's grace in Christ as our great hope (James 2:1; 4:6). Self-reliance will not work. Our solution is not to be left alone with God's law to try harder to be good. It is not to pull ourselves up by our bootstraps, take the bull by the horns, and make ourselves better people by sheer willpower. If there is anything James has told us, it is that we are a terrible mess. Our hope is not in ourselves—our resourcefulness, wisdom, or determination. James says that the solution is God's grace. "But He gives more grace. Therefore He says: 'God resists the proud, but gives grace to the humble'" (James 4:6).

But grace is an often misunderstood idea. Sometimes people mistakenly equate grace with cheap grace or a license to sin and a cloak for covetousness. Others think of grace as about salvation only. Others aren't used to thinking of grace as a spiritual issue at all. What does the Bible mean when it speaks of grace? And what does James mean when he says that grace is the solution to the sin and strife that so easily entangle us?

God's Grace in Salvation

It is important to understand what grace is—unmerited favor from God. Grace means different things to different people, but the Bible has a particular perspective on it. When someone says that a person performed a gymnastic routine with a lot of grace, they are referring to skill and poise. When someone "says grace" over a meal, it means they prayed over it. But when the Bible refers to grace, it often is speaking of God's saving people from sin, and the word highlights the fact that salvation is not bestowed on sinners because they deserve it in any way. Grace is by nature undeserved. God saves people who are totally unworthy of it and actually deserve quite the opposite, condemnation.

It's often the case that we learn best by seeing how common ideas fit together into a larger whole. Are we saved by grace, by faith, or by Christ? The Bible says we are saved by all three. Ephesians 2:8 says we are saved "by grace" and "through faith." Second Corinthians 5:18 says that God "reconciled us to Himself through Jesus Christ." Someone might ask, "Well, which of the three is it?" There is no contradiction in saying that we are saved by all three; they all work together beautifully to create a rich picture of salvation.

God tells us that Christians are "justified freely by His grace" (Rom. 3:24). *Justified* refers to God's declaring a sinner to be righteous. When He does so, He frees them from condemnation, when they believe the gospel of Christ (Rom. 5:1). The word *freely* means "without a cause." In other words, the grace of salvation is not bestowed because of any worthiness in the person receiving it. In fact, bringing in the concept of worth destroys the very idea of grace. Sinners have fallen short of God's glory and deserve wrath and judgment: "the wages of sin is death" (Rom. 6:23). To receive favor when one is full of sin and deserving of wrath, that is grace! Salvation is of grace alone, because those who receive it deserve wrath alone. This is important to understand lest we presume that God owes us or that we are worthy of His love. No, salvation is unmerited, or undeserved. We are saved by grace.

God also tells us we are saved by Christ. We are justified "through the redemption that is in Christ Jesus" and "by His blood" (Rom. 3:24; 5:9). This is important to understand lest we think that our faith is the basis on which God shows us grace, as if God owes us because we did the work of believing. That is an error called Neonomianism, which makes faith into a new law to keep for salvation. The basis on which believers receive salvation is not faith; it is the person and work of Jesus Christ. Christ's righteous life and sacrificial death provide a legal basis for saving sinners. God doesn't unjustly pardon people who deserve judgment. He will by no means clear the guilty (Ex. 34:7). Unjustly pardoning is like a judge letting a murderer off the hook. Such a judge is hardly good and just. But God doesn't unjustly pardon like this when He saves people from their sins and declares ungodly people righteous. Redemption comes about because of Christ, "whom God set forth as a propitiation" (Rom. 3:25). A propitiation is an appeasement of wrath. The penalty of death was God's wrath against sin, but Christ appeased the wrath because He paid the penalty. He suffered in the place of sinners, enduring their curse (Gal. 3:13). Grace comes to us because of Christ alone. Without Him as our mediator and surety, we would have only wrath. Therefore, we are saved by Christ in the sense that He, as our surety and substitute, provides a basis for our salvation by His righteous life and His death on the cross.

God also tells us we are saved by faith. As we just saw, faith is not the basis on which sinners receive grace and are saved, but it is the instrument by which God gives saving grace to them. We are saved by faith alone in the sense that the instrumental cause of our salvation is faith, not our good works. God wants sinners to cast away all confidence in their actions and depend on Christ alone. This is important lest we think that we do anything to be saved. On the contrary, salvation is not by works but by faith (Eph. 2:8–9).

We've alluded to different sorts of causes in salvation. There are ultimate causes, efficient causes, and instrumental causes (or means). These are distinct categories of thought about causation that have been around a long time. When discussing salvation, these areas helpfully explain why the Bible speaks of various things as causing salvation. God's grace is the ultimate cause of our salvation, faith is the instrumental cause, and Christ is the efficient cause.

People today often do not specify various ways to understand causation, so here is a plain illustration that uses all three concepts in a concrete scenario we all can relate to; the illustration falls short but might help you understand how grace functions in a larger system of salvation. If you need to go to the emergency room for an IV infusion of saline in order to avoid death by severe dehydration, there will be several causes of your rehydration. First, there is the doctor's willingness to administer the saline. Second, there is the saline itself, which is what your body needs. And third, there is the IV apparatus, or the instrument by which the saving saline is administered. The ultimate cause of your rehydration is the ER doctor administering the saline. The effective cause of your rehydration is the saline. The instrument that delivers the saline is the IV. No one in their right mind would object to someone saying that you were helped by the doctor, by the saline, and by the IV. There is no contradiction; all three have essential parts to play, and it is important to keep them distinct so that each is seen in its proper function. To apply this illustration to the matter at hand, God's gracious heart is the ultimate reason you receive favor, not any merit on your part. Christ, His righteous life and atoning death, is the effective cause, not your choice or faith. Faith in Christ alone is the instrumental cause, not your works. God gives you that faith (Phil. 1:29), and with it comes justification. To use the illustration again, the saline has the elements your body must have, but you cannot have it without connecting to the IV. Believing the gracious gospel is the means to receive Christ, whom your soul so desperately needs. As John Flavel said, "It is true, the death of Christ is the meritorious cause of remission, but faith is the instrumental applying cause; and as Christ's blood is necessary in its place, so is our faith in its place also."[1]

Christ is what our soul needs, and it is faith in Him that derives the benefit from Him. Christ's person—of two natures, one fully human and one fully divine—is what we need. Christ provides us a new humanity in which we can share, one distinct from that of Adam. Christ, the second Adam, is not changeable as the first Adam was. Adam was tempted and fell in the garden, bringing all his descendants into ruin with him. But Christ overcame temptation and gives His righteousness to believers forever. Because Christ is God, His righteousness is not like Adam's changeable righteousness. Christ's is immutable, everlasting, and not subject to corruption. His righteous life as the God-man is imputed to those who trust Him so that it can be said they have "the righteousness of God" (2 Cor. 5:21). It was His humanity that made it possible for Him to die; it was His deity that gives His death efficacy for all believers throughout

---

1. John Flavel, "The Fountain of Life," in *The Works of John Flavel* (1820; repr., Edinburgh: Banner of Truth, 1982), 1:151.

time. Faith sees all these things; it seizes on Christ's person and work and takes rest in them. Faith connects the needy, dying sinner to the perfect life-giving Savior, and both faith and the Savior are gifts from the gracious heart of God.

Someone might wonder how this discussion of grace, Christ, and faith are related to the practical matter of healing contentious relationships. Here is the point to which all this is heading: when we realize we are saved by grace alone, through faith alone, and because of Christ alone, we begin to realize that, in ourselves, we really are wretches and totally unable to add a whit to our salvation. We realize we truly are spiritually impoverished and must give glory to God alone for salvation. Without seeing ourselves as total beggars in need of grace, it is all too likely that our relationship with God will lack the humility and awed gratitude that sinners like us should have when coming to a holy and merciful God. It is too easy to come to God thinking highly of ourselves—of our works, will-power, choices, or wisdom. It is this sort of sinful pride that leads people to exalt themselves and create strife. If we have pride at the center and starting point of our relationship with God, it is no wonder contention is present in our lives. We must recognize that we are spiritual beggars, deserving of never-ending wrath and yet marvelously graced with eternal life with God through Christ. Realizing how indebted we are to God's grace will humble us into the posture of needy supplicants, just the sort of people whom God looks to help (Isa. 66:2). Accepting salvation as utterly gracious humbles us—or at least it should—and humble people seek help in God and find it.

Sanctifying Grace for the Humble

Grace is of at least two sorts: justifying grace and sanctifying grace. Paul speaks of justifying grace when he says, "By grace you have been saved through faith, and that not of yourselves; it is the gift of God, not of works, lest anyone should boast" (Eph. 2:8–9). He also highlights sanctifying grace, saying, "By the grace of God I am what I am, and His grace toward me was not in vain; but I labored more abundantly than they all, yet not I, but the grace of God which was with me" (1 Cor. 15:10).

In this second verse Paul is quick to explain that his hard work as an apostle was not due to himself. He doesn't want to take any credit for his labors. Paul's passion was to give God glory for all things. His lifelong labors, he insists, were due to God's grace. He's essentially saying that his sanctification is due to God's unmerited favor. The implication is that grace is not something we leave behind after we're saved and justified; God keeps pouring it on us throughout our lives, and all of our progress is due to His continued generosity. Whether you're thinking of our entrance into the Christian life or of every moment in that life, grace rules. We breathe an atmosphere of grace, run under a sky of grace, swim in an ocean of grace. Pick your metaphor, as long as you see your gracious God everywhere and your heavenly Father's hand upholding you from first to last.

James 4:6 is speaking of this sanctifying grace. This fact is evident when he says, "but He gives *more* grace," for Christians need continuing supplies of grace to deal with the problems of sin that they experience. This is naturally what you would expect given that James is writing his letter to Christians, or those who have already trusted in Christ. James is speaking of continual supplies of unmerited favor from God to help us in our daily struggles against sin. Whether or not this ministers comfort and inspiration to you reveals your spiritual state. People who rely on themselves do not find it good news. Those who trust in the arm of flesh do not rejoice in God's grace for power in the Christian life. But people who feel their weakness and frailty, who are keenly aware that they are an abyss of spiritual needs, will find James's news to be a reinvigorating breath of air from heaven.

This truth of God's giving more grace meets a need in our lives we may not be aware we have. God gives continual supplies of grace and isn't insensitive to the fact that His children have continuing struggles. He never says, "I've helped you enough" or "Haven't you worn out your welcome coming to Me?" The apostle John tells us that all believers have received of Christ's fullness and "grace for grace," or grace on top of grace (John 1:16). That means there is a never-ending supply of mercy and help in Christ. He is an ever-flowing fountain of life. Blessing just keeps welling up out of Christ's generous heart. James promises that God gives more grace; we can come to God for help and never feel rebuffed by Him or that the throne of grace is empty or that the fountain of life has dried up.

If you have taken to heart what James has said in 4:1–5, then you have stopped pointing fingers at other people and are blaming yourself for your own sin. You've realized the depth of your unfaithfulness to God, and you've seen how it has wreaked havoc in your relationships. You've pridefully exalted your desires over God and others, and you have caused contention and strife when you didn't get what you wanted. Now you may be at a loss about how to deal with it all. Getting a good look at the depravity of your heart might even make you wonder if you'll ever be able to change. James assures us that sanctifying grace is available to us, and he quotes an Old Testament verse to prove it: "God gives grace to the humble" (Prov. 3:34). How should we respond to this? We should simply believe it's true that God gives sanctifying grace to us so that we can overcome sin. Do you believe that God offers gracious empowerment to overcome your sin? Believing this in any legitimate way means accepting you don't have power to overcome it on your own. People don't flee to God for help with any urgency until they've despaired of themselves. But if you sense your inability, do you believe there is hope in Christ for your sin problems? Are you willing to call out to Him for help against strife? Will you say no to despair and depend on the Lord?

Once you have accepted that you need God's sanctifying grace to help you overcome your sin and stop contributing to the strife around you, a question is raised. How can I get this grace from God? I see my great need of it; I believe it is real and available, but I need access to the throne of grace to get help in my time of need (Heb. 4). How can I come to God and get the help I need against my evil heart and bad habits? It isn't as simple as praying to God. The proverb James quotes says that God gives grace to the humble. If we want sanctifying grace when we come to God, we must abandon the pride that exalted our desires to the place of rivals to God. This is simply to say that we must repent once more. We must thoroughly hate our sin and flee to God for help against it.

I fear that many don't gain grace to overcome strife because they don't really hate their sin. Imagine a person asking you this interesting question: "What would you do if you had a sin problem that had a stranglehold on you, and you pled with

God over and over to take it away, but He never did, like Paul and his thorn in the flesh?" Imagine that this person did indeed have a terrible sin problem, and it was so entrenched that it had been partially responsible for destroying his most important relationships. But when he asks you this, do you sense anything wrong with his question? It seems as if he were implicitly blaming God for his sin, doesn't it? It seems he is doubting the reality of empowering grace from God too. How should you reply? For one thing, Paul's thorn in the flesh was not a sin problem but a physical malady. Paul was not referring to sin problems when he said that he gloried in his infirmities (2 Cor. 12:9–10)! Also, if I were consistently falling into persistent sin, I hope I would assume that I don't hate my sin enough and that I'm still tolerating it, justifying it, pointing fingers at others, excusing myself. I would get on my face, cry out in sorrow for my sin, and ask God to give me a true loathing of it. This is what James is saying when he calls us to be humble to get empowering grace. Do you want power over sin? Then come to God humbly, rejecting the pride that has caused you to exalt your desires and cause strife.

Some people don't hate their sin enough, while others do hate it but are quailing in fear at its ferocity and are tempted to despair at it. Someone once asked me what I would say to a person who was depressed over his continued struggle with sin. He genuinely hated sin but continually committed it, and it was discouraging him. It was making him have serious doubts about his spiritual condition. It would be easy to say to such a person, "Stop looking at yourself and just look at Christ's perfection." Of course he should look at Christ's perfection; that is crucial because grace comes from knowing Christ, and nothing empowers the soul more than a good long look at Christ in His mediatorial offices in behalf of sinners. But the same Christ to whom we should look also gives His Holy Spirit, who then graciously empowers believers in their fight against sin (Gal. 5:16). This empowerment is so significant that the apostle expects and even insists that Christians demonstrate a change of life (Titus 3:8). No Christian should ever feel helpless and at the mercy of his lusts (Rom. 6:14). Christians should feel empowered to wage war against sin in their lives, and they should expect substantial victory. They should strive and find much success in overcoming the world (1 John 5:4). When this person asked me this question, two passages came to mind that can help anyone who is in a battle to the death with sin and fears losing. First is Peter's reply to Jesus when Jesus asked if he wanted to leave Him: "Lord, to whom shall we go? You have the words of eternal life" (John 6:68). Peter had reached the point of placing all his hope in this one person, Jesus Christ. When you are struggling against sin, the first thing is to be assured that there is no help or hope in anyone but Christ, so don't entertain any doubt of His willingness and ability to give empowerment. All your eggs must be in this basket—all hope is in Him alone. He is your answer. The second is Jacob's reply to the angel when asked to be let go: "I will not let You go unless You bless me!" (Gen. 32:26). Jacob is seldom a good example, but he certainly is on this occasion. He shows almost a stubborn, holy insistence on gaining blessing from God. It is this quality that caused him to gain the name Israel, "prevailer with God." This is the way to prevail—to see God in Christ as the only hope and then seek Him for help with a holy, importunate insistence. If you are downcast over your sin, take these two scriptural statements together, forging an iron-hard alloy that imparts a steadfast faith in God's willingness and ability to sanctify you and an undying resolve to seek holiness at His hand. As Juan de Avila said, "Woe to that soul which presumes to think that he can approach God in any other way than as a sinner asking mercy. Know yourself to be wicked, and God will wrap you up warm in the mantle of his goodness."[2]

Study Questions

1. What verses in James show that he is not "legal"—that is, he is not offering bare commands to be obeyed without divine help as our answer to sin problems?

2. What is grace?

3. What does it mean that we are saved by grace? How does this fit with the truth that we are saved by Christ and saved by faith?

4. How does knowing we are saved by grace help in fighting sin and strife?

5. What is sanctifying grace? How do we know James is referring to sanctifying grace in James 4:6?

2. Juan de Avila, quoted in *Expositor's Greek Testament*, ed. W. Robertson Nicoll (repr., Peabody, Mass.: Hendrickson, 2002), 5:172.

6. Why is James's statement "but He gives more grace" comforting and encouraging?

7. How should we seek God for continuing supplies of sanctifying grace?

8. When we continue falling into sin, instead of blaming God for not empowering us, what should we do?

9. Should any Christian feel helpless and at the mercy of his lusts?

10. What sort of attitude should we have about God and His grace when we find ourselves continuing to commit sins we hate?

CHAPTER 4

Come to God in
Humble Repentance

*Therefore submit to God. Resist the devil and he will flee
from you. Draw near to God and He will draw near to you.
Cleanse your hands, you sinners; and purify your hearts, you
double-minded.*

—JAMES 4:7–8

To gain sanctifying grace from God in our fight against sin and
strife, we must feel our need of it, believe that grace is truly
available, and seek it from God humbly in true repentance.
James now goes into detail explaining what that humble repentance looks like. He fleshes it out so that we can compare our
own hearts with what true repentance is. Notice the connec-
tion between verses 6 and 7—James says God gives grace to
the humble, and then he adds, "Therefore submit to God." He's
explaining how we should respond in light of who God is; he's
explaining how to come to God for sanctifying grace. We may
be failing to receive power against sin and strife because we
aren't coming to God humbly.

James wants us to gain the grace necessary to overcome our
sinful strife. So what does humbly coming to God for grace
against sin look like? Are we truly humbled or are we actually

still perpetuating our self-exalting ways? James describes several facets of a humble and repentant seeking of God for grace against sin. These are wonderful helps in understanding how to relate as a wretched sinner to a generous and gracious God.

Submit to God

First, we must submit ourselves to God. Since God resists the proud but gives grace to the humble, submission is required if we want grace. James uses a word for submission that means "to arrange oneself under" or "to subordinate oneself to." It is quite natural for him to tell us to subordinate ourselves to God; our problem is that we have exalted our desires so much that we have sinned against God for them. We have maximized our desires and minimized God, so we must repent of this and reverse our course. We must put God in His rightful place as Lord and place ourselves under Him. God must be on the throne, and we must bow before it.

The mind has the capacity to concentrate or prioritize, and by focusing on God, or putting Him at the center of our thinking, other things are naturally moved to its margins. The reverse is also true; if we focus our attentions on other things, God gets marginalized. If we concentrate on some issue (even a theological one!)—a relationship that we worry over or an activity we love—we marginalize God. God must be first and foremost. Sometimes people can get very confused about this, because they cannot imagine thinking about God when their job requires their complete attention for much of the day, for example. But this is really less of a problem than it seems, because the concept of centrality merely illustrates an important truth. The question is not simply a matter of how much direct attention you give God. Putting God first is a matter of involvement as well as attention. God must not merely be central, He must be everywhere. He must have the central place in our lives, but He also must connect with everything in them (2 Cor. 10:5).

Here is the question in a nutshell: Is God central in your life, and do you involve Him in everything? Here are some thoughts to help you examine yourself on this: If you cannot bring yourself to read the Bible for any length of time, you are not putting God at the center of life, even for a little while in private worship. If you downplay His ordinances, you aren't putting Him at the center of public worship. If you ignore one of His commands, you are marginalizing His authority to rule you. These are three areas in which it is helpful to see whether you are making Him central. Now let's think about making God ubiquitous in your life. If you want to enjoy God's world without thanking Him, you're not letting Him touch every blessing. If you try to accomplish things without prayer of dependence on Him, you're not letting Him touch every goal and accomplishment. Submission to God means returning Him to His proper place as being our central focus and as connected to every aspect of life; this involves moving our desires to their proper, subordinate place. If we exalt our desires over Him, that is pride, and strife will result. It is unnerving to think of all the ways the soul can go astray. Thank God that He gives grace to help repentant sinners! We ought to seek God's grace even to help us seek Him for grace! He is the answer to our every need, and even if our prayer is an inarticulate, garbled cry, He will help.

Submitting to God is especially important when we suffer discouragement or when a circumstance dashes our expectations and we feel everything is against us, as Jacob experienced (Gen. 42:36). Never will you be more tempted to become bitter and rail against people and even against God. When setbacks abound, strife and abuse are not far off. At such times, James's words are especially relevant. Recognize your tendency to care more about yourself and your desires than about Christ. Accept that it may even be true that you follow Him just to get what you want. Be aware of your adulterous heart. Admit your corrupt nature, which exalts self. See your sinful nature as the enemy it is, and soundly reject it, taking God's side instead of your own. Humbly bow your knee to your Lord who suffered and died for you and who richly deserves your first love and loyalty. If you come to God in this way, you are truly repenting and can be assured that God, who gives grace to the humble, will give grace to you, for you are truly submitting to Him. He doesn't help the proud; in fact, He resists them! You must submit to God humbly and grant Him His rightful place in your life.

Resist the Devil

Second, we must resist the devil. This is the flip side of submitting to God. If we truly submit to God, then we are by nature resisting His enemy, the devil. Is your life full of strife and contention? If you answer yes, the devil has been living in your midst, throwing an infernal party, as it were. You've been there in the midst of it all, contributing to "confusion and every evil thing" (James 3:16). James is telling us to reverse this. He assures us that submitting to God will result in driving away the enemy.

You may not like to think that causing strife is surrendering to the devil, but Paul clearly explains that each Christian struggles against "the wiles of the devil" and against "principalities" and "powers" (Eph. 6:10–12). It is quite possible (probable? inevitable?) for Christians to sin, do wrong, and fall into ways promoted by the enemy. Strife is one of those ways. Accept that when you sinned, you were a child of God who fell temporarily into the ways of the devil. If anything will wake you up to your state, seeing your behavior as linked to the devil will. James hints that these are indeed the stakes when he says that strife is "earthly, sensual, demonic" (James 3:15). Let's put it in a way that fits with James's blunt style—stop fraternizing with the enemy. Resist him before whom you once groveled. Give the devil a "Dear John" letter. And as you do so, be amazed once more that God has mercy on sinners like us. If we soundly reject the devil, we are truly and fervently repenting before God, and we can be assured that His grace is on its way to us. He is so great-hearted to help people who have been disloyal to Him! But how can we expect help if we are still cozying up to God's enemy?

Draw Near to God

Third, we must draw near to God. This assumes that when we fell into strife and contention, we wandered from God and went astray. Repentance means that we must turn around and run back to Him. This too might be a hard pill to swallow, because you may believe that true believers cannot apostatize from God. It is quite right to think that they cannot. People apostatize, but in doing so they show that they were never truly Christians (see 1 John 2:19). True believers in Christ can never fall away and perish (John 10:28). But tragically, Christians can and do go astray, backslide, and fall into sinful patterns of life. We must see our strife and contention for what it is: a wandering from God. God never moved away from us. Even while we wandered, He was ensuring that goodness and mercy still followed us all our days. He was there ensuring that all things, even our sinful wandering, would work together for our good! But we still wandered. We still went astray. You must turn around and turn back to your Father with zeal, like the prodigal who came to himself and ran home to his father.

James promises that if we draw near to God, He will draw near to us. Again, it is not that God abandoned us when we wandered from Him. Nothing in the present or the future can separate us from God's love (Rom. 8:38–39). When Christ died, all our sins were nailed to the cross, even our future ones (Col. 2:13–14). This means that there can be no skeleton tumbling from the closet that will cause God to recoil and reject us. Our sin is old news to God. When we went astray we were just as saved as when we submit ourselves to God. God's love and nearness do not depend on our performance, and it is crucial that we understand that, or we will fall into a subtle form of works salvation and begin thinking that our acceptance with God depends on ourselves.

Nevertheless, though God does not abandon His children, He does chasten them. It is a sign of His fatherly care (Heb. 12:5–6). When God does chasten us, it can be difficult, and He can seem distant and alienated from us (cf. Ps. 10:1). It may even seem that He has removed His attention and help (Ps. 66:18). But when He does, He is not rejecting us but rather disciplining us to bring us to repentance. James is telling us that if we want God to return to us, hear us, empower us, and strengthen us once more, we must turn from our wandering and come back to Him. Calvin noted that "God is never wanting to us, except when we alienate ourselves from him."[1] If you find your heart longing to run to Christ in sorrow for the strife you've caused, you should raise your heart to thank Him for continuing His good work in you (Phil. 1:6). You wouldn't have the desire if He hadn't already been working graciously in your soul. If you are dismayed at your lack of desire for repentance and for God, cry out with David, "Create in me a clean heart, O God" (Ps. 51:10). We must seek all things from Him, even our change of heart and obedience to His Word.

How do you draw near to God? Hebrews 4:14–16 speaks of coming boldly to the throne of grace in light of the perfect high priesthood of Christ. In other words, drawing near to God does not mean coming in our own names, in our own persons, thinking we'll be accepted simply because we are sorry and are coming. No, there is no relationship with God without the one Mediator between God and man (1 Tim. 2:5). Drawing near to God means coming to Him humbly repentant but also depending on our perfect and compassionate mediator Jesus Christ for acceptance with God, for Christ ever lives to make intercession for us and to save us to the uttermost. Christ is central to all aspects of life, and we must not think of drawing near to God without thinking of Christ's role as mediator.

Thus far James has defined repentance as submitting to God, or putting God back in His proper place of lordship; resisting His enemy the devil; and coming back from our wandering to God through Christ. But James has more to say about how to come humbly to God for sanctifying grace.

---

1. Calvin, *Commentaries on the Epistle of James*, 334.

Cleanse Your Hands

Fourth, we must cleanse our hands. James refers to our hands to point out that repentance affects our actions. It is true that we must focus on the heart since that is where evil proceeds (Mark 7:21–22). But evil hearts do not produce evil in the abstract; they produce evil deeds. Our actions must be purified every bit as much as our hearts. God cares about what our bodies do just as much as He cares about our motives and our feelings. Otherwise, why would He tell us to present our bodies to Him as instruments of righteousness (Rom. 6:13)? The heart is primary, since it is the source, but the fruits of the heart are deeds. Therefore, our actions must become conformed to God's Word. We must become obedient: "If you love Me, keep My commandments" (John 14:15).

Someone once said that if you sow a thought, you'll reap an action. If you sow an action, you'll reap a habit. If you sow a habit, you'll reap a character. And if you sow a character, you'll reap a destiny. "Whatever a man sows, that he will also reap" (Gal. 6:7). If we have allowed our evil thoughts to manifest themselves in strife and contention, has it become habitual? A habit of making strife, left unopposed, will define your character and your destiny. How vital it is to flee to God with real hatred for sin, seeking His gracious empowerment against it! What we do habitually says everything about us.

This emphasis on change of life is crucial, but there is a subtle danger in it. One does not reform one's life in order to be justified and saved or to keep oneself saved. Yes, a person must repent to be saved (Acts 3:19). But such repentance refers to the initial change of mind, the turning away from sin and clinging to Christ that happens at conversion, not the lengthy sanctification process that purifies the life and makes it more holy by the power of the Spirit. It is crucial to understand this, or you might conclude that salvation is only for those who have cleaned themselves up first. That is nothing more than works salvation. There is no cleansing from sin but that which is found in Jesus's blood. Attempting first to cleanse ourselves just adds to our filth. As Joseph Hart wrote in his hymn "Come, Ye Sinners, Poor and Needy," we must not delude ourselves that we can make ourselves better before coming to Christ:

> Come ye weary, heavy laden,
> Bruised and mangled by the fall;
> If you tarry till you're better,
> You will never come at all:
> Not the righteous,
> Not the righteous,
> Not the righteous—
> Sinners Jesus came to call.
>
> Let not conscience make you linger,
> Nor of fitness fondly dream;
> All the fitness he requireth
> Is to feel your need of him;
> This he gives you,
> This he gives you,
> This he gives you—
> 'Tis the Spirit's rising beam.

It is also important to realize that true faith in Christ always results in transformation of life. There is no true salvation where there is no transformation (James 2). But we must not think to seek this change in order to be saved! We must seek to change as gratitude for being saved. Sanctification is to be a joyous affair of trust in Christ and His salvation, even as we strive. Sanctification happens through conscious dependence on union with Christ and the power of the Holy Spirit (Rom. 6:1–11; Gal. 5:16). To attempt to change without depending on the gracious means that God has provided would be like trying to breathe without lungs or see without eyes. Union with Christ and the filling of the Spirit are as necessary to Christian growth as eyes are to seeing. Yes, we must work to be holy, but we must confidently cling to our all-sufficient Savior every step of the way. Otherwise we will engage in our duties in a legal way, as if all it takes is determination and willpower. Without Him we can do nothing that pleases God, so we must seek to cleanse our hands and reform our lives in dependence on His provision, going forward on our knees and rejoicing in the victory He has promised in Christ (Rom. 6:14). He is our only hope for progress in sanctification. When James says we must cleanse our hands, he is not implying that we can do that on our own. He knows we need Christ and the Spirit.

If we find that sin has gotten a foothold in, or a stranglehold on, our actions, we must see it and confess it. If strife is something we still often or regularly cause, we must not "lie against the truth" (James 3:14). Anytime we fall easily before the onslaught of our desires, we are in critical condition. If we cannot keep from sinning, we have a severe problem that must be immediately addressed. Anytime we cannot gain the upper hand in our struggle against sin, we are failing to experience the victory over the world that God has given believers (1 John 5:4). You must cleanse your hands. This does not mean you must make efforts at self-reformation. John Owen said, "Mortification from a self-strength, carried on by ways of self-invention, to the end of a self-righteousness, is the soul and substance of all false religion in the world."[2] We do not cleanse our hands by self-effort, self-discipline, or ingenuity. We must flee once again to Christ's blood for cleansing, even if we've fallen a thousand times. We must trust Him to give us the victory He's promised. We must be like Jacob, who wouldn't let Him go until He blessed him (Gen. 32:26). We must commit ourselves to God's supply of the Spirit of God (Gal. 5:16).

Once your faith is fixed on Christ for victory over sin, arise from your bondage and walk away from your chains, resolving with a joyful and free heart to walk in His ways. You will not have complete victory in this life, but He does promise massive and substantial victory (Rom. 6:14). If you are a believer, the Spirit's empowerment is your birthright, so take it. Cleanse your hands, you sinners!

Purify Your Hearts

Finally, we must purify our hearts. Before we can change our actions, we must have a changed heart. Without this crucial order, true change doesn't occur. Any "change" that is merely imposed from without is really just Pharisaism, which cleans the outside of the cup and leaves the inside filthy (Matt. 23:25). External change without a new heart is an evil. As Calvin said, "Learn what is the true character of repentance. It is not only an outward amendment of life, but its beginning is the cleansing of the heart. It is also necessary, on the other hand, that the

---

2. John Owen, *The Mortification of Sin* (1656; repr., Edinburgh: Banner of Truth, 2007), 3.

fruits of inward repentance should appear in the uprightness of our works."[3]

Sometimes people fear making efforts at outward change because they don't have a heart to obey; they fear being Pharisees. They are honest enough to admit that they do not want to obey, but they use this spiritual deadness as an excuse to do nothing. I fear they think there are only two options—heartless obedience or inactivity. But this is a fallacy. We do not have to either sit and do nothing or work with a dead heart, for God promises to continue the good work He has begun in believers, and He promises to work in them both to desire and to do His good pleasure (Phil. 1:6; 2:13). With promises like these, we can be assured that there is a glorious third option—Spirit-empowered obedience from a changed heart that is gloriously free. To remain in inactivity is to deny that God can and does change the heart. To use heartlessness as an excuse not to serve is to deny the promises of God. It is to say that God has stopped giving the desire to obey.

The psalmists often prayed for God to carry out such inward work. They were always asking Him to perform spiritual heart surgery on them. They felt they didn't fear God enough, so they prayed, "Unite my heart to fear Your name" (Ps. 86:11). They felt ignorant of the extent of their evil hearts, so they pleaded with God, "Cleanse me from secret faults" (Ps. 19:12). They felt unable to deal with the depravity of their hearts, so they cried out, "Create in me a clean heart, O God" (Ps. 51:10). This is how to gain a clean heart that loves God and wants to obey. And when we by faith depend on His inward working

---

3. Calvin, *Epistle of James*, 335.

to purify us by His blood, we can confidently walk forward to serve God with bold deeds, knowing He will renew our love, empower us, make up for our lack, and make our imperfect deeds acceptable in our perfect High Priest (1 Peter 2:5).

How do we seek God for empowering grace against sin? So far James has said several things: we must submit to God as Lord and no longer exalt our desires over Him; resist the devil and no longer fraternize with the enemy; draw near to God and return from our wandering; cleanse our hands, giving attention to change of actions; and purify our hearts, seeking for change in our souls by God's grace. In short, there is no sincere seeking of God's empowering grace without striving after these things. This is what it looks like to seek God's help against sin.

James is not finished explaining what it looks like to come to God humbly to get grace to conquer sin. In the next chapter, we'll see that he adds a remarkably experiential matter— sorrowing over our sin.

Study Questions

1. What five qualities are crucial in seeking God's help to overcome sin and strife?

2. Does putting God first and keeping Him in your awareness while attending to necessary tasks seem impossible? Think how you might do so while performing tasks like doing your schoolwork, fixing the brakes on the car, or sitting up at night with a sick baby.

3. Do you feel the need to ask God to help you seek His sanctifying grace? Why or why not?

4. What does it mean to resist the devil? What does it mean to draw near to God?

5. Why is it important to understand that God's love for us does not depend on our performance?

6. Why should sorrow over the sin and strife we've cause lead to joy in Christ?

7. Is it a comfort to know that growth in your Christian life is a result of union with Christ and the work of the Holy Spirit rather than your own effort?

8. The psalmists, who wrote inspired Scripture, felt the need to implore God to graciously enable them to obey. Do you share their sense of need and their desire? How would you know if you do?

CHAPTER 5

A Place for Humble Sorrow

Lament and mourn and weep! Let your laughter be turned to mourning and your joy to gloom. Humble yourselves in the sight of the Lord, and He will lift you up.
—JAMES 4:9–10

In these verses James informs us of the need for sorrow, then he explains how sorrow manifests itself in our demeanor. James is essentially showing us that coming humbly as a sinner to God and seeking grace for empowerment involves something emotionally—mourning over our sin. If we've fallen into sin, we cannot humbly seek God for grace without sorrow over what we've done.

Experiencing Sorrow

First, James tells us that we must be afflicted, mourn, and weep. Without real sorrow for sin, we do not experience real repentance. If you've never cared that you have sinned and fallen short of the glory of God, you've never repented. Saying you have repented but never feeling sorrow over your sin is like saying you've eaten but never opened your mouth. It may be that there are many people in Christian circles who have never actually repented and come into Christ's true church. John Bunyan called such vain profession *presumption*: "Presumption, then, is that which severs faith and repentance, concluding that the soul shall be saved by grace, though the man was never made sorry for sin."[1]

Repenting and turning away from sin to God is a repudiation and rejection of sin. It is an emotional reaction against it that involves dismay and chagrin for having committed it. It is like saying in horror, "No! What have I done?" Some people are by nature unemotional, while others feel a whole range of emotions all the time. But our personalities are irrelevant to this issue—whether you are an iceberg or a volcano, to repent you must feel sorrow for sin.

James is telling us that continued sorrowful repentance is necessary for empowerment against sin and strife; if we want deliverance from the sin that so easily ensnares us, we must get real. We must really loathe, confess, and turn away from sin, and we must feel the remorse of a person who has perpetrated evil and hates it.

If you fear that you've never felt sorrow for sin, get alone with God and confess your hard heart. Do it right now. Tell God you've sinned by not caring that you've sinned. Fearing you've never felt sorrow for sin is a good step toward feeling sorrow for sin. Ask God to give you sorrow. Don't accept feeling sorry for yourself, which is a common but false substitute for true godly sorrow. Consider how your sins have hurt

1. John Bunyan, *The Jerusalem Sinner Saved* (1688; repr., Edinburgh: Banner of Truth, 2005), 86.

others. Place yourself in their shoes. Recognize that your sin has detracted from God's glory. See your sin for the ugly thing that it is. Read passages of Scripture where people are confronted about their terrible sins (2 Sam. 12). Read passages that describe true repentance (Ps. 51; James 4:9; 2 Cor. 7:10–11).

Sometimes people can grasp the importance of godly sorrow and then begin to make pronouncements about how much sorrow a person must express before their repentance should be considered real. This is a mistake. We must not take it on ourselves to dictate how much sorrow is necessary and what forms sorrow should take. It is enough to say that repentance includes true sorrow over sin, and without sorrow, repentance is not genuine. It is enough to say "mourn and weep," just as James says. It may be that the Lord allows you to continue struggling with sin because you have not come to this crucial point of refraining from accusing others and simply mourning and sorrowing over the sin you yourself have caused. You still struggle because you don't hate sin.

If we honestly evaluate our repentance, we will discover faults with it. It is crucial to recognize that our salvation does not depend on the quality of our repentance. It depends on the perfect obedience and effective atonement of Jesus Christ. You may struggle with fear because you are afraid that your repentance and faith aren't good enough. You may wonder if you've really attained a genuine conversion experience. But who is to say when your faith and repentance have reached the undefinable level of "good enough"? Is it not true that thinking that you must attain a certain "level" is uncomfortably close to works salvation? Yes, you must repent and believe, but these things are not a new form of works righteousness. Christ is our righteousness

(1 Cor. 1:30). And Jesus accepts our imperfect faith, since nothing we do is perfect. Everything we do, including our faith and repentance, is marred by imperfection. When Jesus spoke to a man whose son was demon possessed, He told the man to believe and his son would be made well. The man responded, "I believe; help my unbelief!" (Mark 9:24). Jesus did not turn the man away saying, "Come back to Me when you can express a stronger faith." He accepted the man's weak faith and healed his son. One of the glorious things about Christ is that He makes up for our deficiencies, which are never-ending. If you come to God and cry out to Him, "Save me, I'm Yours. Help my hard heart. Forgive my dry eyes," He will hear and He will save. Our repentance must be genuine and include true sorrow over sin, but we must not rely on our repentance—such a weak foundation! Trust in Christ alone. As Augustus Toplady wrote,

> Not the labors of my hands
> Can fulfil thy law's demands;
> Could my zeal no respite know,
> Could my tears forever flow,
> All for sin could not atone;
> Thou must save, and thou alone.[2]

Sorrow Affects Demeanor

Second, true sorrow affects demeanor; we must let our laughter be turned to mourning and our joy to heaviness. This tests whether one is truly sorrowful. Have the external trappings of happiness been removed and replaced with expressions of sorrow? Have we come to feel sickened at the thought of being

---

2. Augustus Toplady, "Rock of Ages, Cleft for Me."

frivolous? Have we realized that our sin is too heinous for light-heartedness? Has flippancy become nauseatingly inappropriate in light of the gravity of sin? Has the thought of a party become to you like the thought of laughing in a leprosy ward? Perhaps a better metaphor is that of joking at the deathbed of someone you are responsible for hurting. Repentance ought to involve sorrow, which is proved real when lightness evaporates to be replaced with grief over the harm you've caused.

Though it is undoubtedly true that a person can fake any emotion, true repentance really does have external manifestations. In the Old Testament, when God sent the prophet to preach judgment to Nineveh, they truly repented. "The people of Nineveh believed God, proclaimed a fast, and put on sackcloth, from the greatest to the least of them" (Jonah 3:5). They believed God's message of judgment and therefore repented, and their repentance had external manifestations. They abstained from food. They put on sackcloth, which was a rough, uncomfortable garment associated with mourning. They gave up common comforts and enjoyments because they had become convinced of their sin and of God's coming judgment.

It may seem extreme to stop laughing and start lamenting. But really it is the most appropriate response to the sin and strife we cause. We do evil, and it is only right that our smiles disappear when we realize it. How can we hurt people and go on our merry way? How can we dishonor God and laugh? It is not unreasonable to think that smiles will disappear when the reality of what we've done sinks in. It is not extreme to say that conviction hasn't occurred till you stop smiling and you mourn over the sin you have committed and the pain you have caused.

How Sorrow and Rejoicing Relate

Someone might wonder how sorrowing and rejoicing can coexist. We are told to rejoice in the Lord always (Phil. 4:4), but here in James we are told to lament over our sin. How can both of these things be? Though joy and sorrow are very different emotions and do not seem to go together, it must be remembered that true repentance does lead to joy in Christ. "Let your laughter be turned to mourning" is not incompatible with "rejoice always" (1 Thess. 5:16). The one leads to the other and is a prerequisite for it. Conviction leads to repentance, and if repentance is mixed with faith in God's grace in Christ, it leads to the joy of our salvation. Avoiding conviction and sorrow actually short circuits the process and avoids joy. How can a person rejoice in God's forgiveness when that person has never felt downcast over sin? The conviction sets up the joy once you realize the breadth and depth and height of God's grace in Christ. Beware of avoiding conviction of sin out of a "biblical" desire to rejoice in Christ.

Perhaps conviction and sorrow (and thus joy in Christ) do not come to you because you do not really understand the seriousness of sin. The Puritan Ralph Venning wrote that sin is an attack, an assault, on God's being, authority, honor, and attributes. When we see it this way, perhaps we'll feel regret and sorrow for committing it. Perhaps we'll discern how our actions reflect poorly on God and are at odds with His glorious person. Venning wrote that sin is attempted theocide, or God-murder. When a sinner dismisses a commandment from God, whose very nature is lordly, that sinner is rejecting the very nature of the lawgiver. Laws are an extension of the Lord who gives them. You cannot separate the Lord from the laws. They are *His* commandments, the very expressions of His soul (see James 2:10–11). To reject them is to reject Him. To wish them away is to wish Him away.

Sin is opposed to God's being, Venning wrote: "Sin makes the sinner wish and endeavor that there might be no God, for sinners are haters of God (Rom. 1:30). As he who hates his brother is a murderer (1 John 3:15), so, as much as in him lies, he who hates God is a murderer of God."[3]

Sin is opposed to God's authority: "Sin…deposes the sovereignty of God as much as in it lies. It will not that the King of kings should be on the throne, and govern this world which he has made…the voice and language of sin is, 'our lips are our own, who is Lord over us?' (Ps. 12:4). It was from hence that the Jews of old said, 'We are lords, we will come no more to thee' (Jer. 2:31). Thus it attempts to dethrone God."[4]

Sin is also opposed to God's honor: "[Sin] denies God's all-sufficiency. As if there were not contentment and satisfaction enough to be had in the enjoyment of God…! Every Prodigal who leaves the Father's house says in effect, it is better to be elsewhere."[5]

In a statement of remarkable power and insight, Venning noted that sin is opposed to all of God's attributes. He remarks that to God's justice sin says, "I dare you to judge me." Sin abuses God's mercy and treats it as common and nonprecious. It mocks God's patience by continuing to practice evil even as He patiently gives room for repentance. Sin thinks little of

3. Ralph Venning, *The Sinfulness of Sin* (1669; repr., Edinburgh: Banner of Truth, 1997), 35–36.

4. Venning, *Sinfulness of Sin*, 31.

5. Venning, *Sinfulness of Sin*, 32.

God's power because it hopes that in the end He will not be able to make good on His threats against it. Sin scorns God's love because it says, in effect, I'd rather have evil than God's love. Sin rebukes God's providence because it always complains when God allows life to become uncomfortable.[6]

Venning's statements help us to see that there is a world of evil in a single act, or thought, of sin. Such an exposé of sin is necessary if we are to see ourselves as we really are and mourn over what we have done. We must see that by sinning we've said to God's justice, "I dare you." We've treated mercy with contempt by choosing to sin yet again. When we've been presented with the choice between sin and God, we've chosen sin and thus poured scorn on God's love and covenant. If this is a true portrait of sin, it is only reasonable that we ought to stop smiling and start lamenting. Have you?

Summary: Humble Yourself before God

James has explained what true humility looks like, and now he sums up everything he has taught in verses 6–10: "Humble yourselves in the sight of the Lord, and He will lift you up" (James 4:10). Note, however, that he adds two new thoughts.

First, he adds the phrase "in the sight of the Lord." Like Jesus before him (e.g., in Matt. 6:1–18), James emphasizes that our religious motions must be focused on God. In Christian circles there are far too many outward displays that are primarily intended to gain people's good opinion. True dealings with God are between the soul and God first and foremost, and often

---

6. Adapted from Venning, *Sinfulness of Sin*, 32. Venning's original quotation is just difficult enough to warrant a paraphrase.

alone. Religion that validates itself by what man thinks is corrupt in God's sight. Religion that seeks to please people is a foul thing to Him. Paul said, "If I still pleased men, I would not be a bondservant of Christ" (Gal. 1:10). Jesus criticized certain very religious people by pointing out that "all their works they do to be seen by men" (Matt. 23:5). He said that seeking praise from people is antithetical to belief in Christ (John 5:44).

Make your relationship with God private, and seek Him with a whole heart that is honest. Stop using religion as a means of self-promotion. That is what James is getting at here. He is not saying there is no corporate element to religious life. He's not saying that public worship is not important. He is also not saying that it is unimportant to take others' thoughts and ideas into account. We don't want to be unkind, undiplomatic, or arrogant. James is saying that our corrupt nature can make religion all about relationship with people. Religion can become a means of gaining prestige, control, acceptance, or influence when it should be about getting right with God and pleasing Him. If you need to get right with God, go to Him directly through your high priest, Jesus Christ, who ever lives to intercede for you before God's throne. Make your life first and foremost about coming humbly to the Father through Jesus the Son. Humble yourself in the sight of God. As R. C. Sproul was fond of saying, live *coram Deo*, before God's face. Think of yourself as standing alone before God, dealing solely with Him.

Second, James promises that God will lift up the person who comes to Him in this way of humility. But what is James referring to? Lifted up from what? It is in such statements that autonomous thinking can find room to interpret things that give space to the flesh. James is certainly not saying that if we humble ourselves before God, He will lift us up from humility! And He will not necessarily lift us up from the consequences of our sin either. Sometimes a person is forgiven, but consequences persist for a long time, as can be seen in David's life (2 Sam. 12:10–15). People far too often seek God merely to gain better circumstances or to avoid the temporal consequences of their sin. Undoubtedly, when he says that God will lift you up, James is referring to the wretched state of disempowerment and sinfulness that caused strife. God will lift you up from the idolatrous condition you were in when you exalted your desires and quarreled with others. James is also referring to the sorrow and gloom he had just insisted was a part of true repentance. In other words, God will lift us out of sorrow. He doesn't want us to mourn over our sin forever. He doesn't want a lifestyle of repentance to equal a lifestyle of gloom. *Semper reformanda* should not be interpreted as implying never-ceasing sorrow.

If we come to Him, allowing ourselves to be convicted and to feel sorrow for our sin, as we should, God will forgive and lift us up to rejoice in Christ. Since we must repent often, we should be led to rejoicing often. This takes one of the most somber aspects of Christianity, sorrow for sin, and weaves joy into it. It is utterly precious to know that God wants Christians' normal state to be one of joy in Christ (Phil. 4:4). Though sometimes a Christian can sin so severely that rushing past conviction and sorrow would be hasty and inappropriate, it is still true that the normal Christian life is one of joy, and even heinous sinners can achieve a measure of joy in Christ in this life.

Perhaps the consequences of your sin are so hard and so long-standing that you feel you will never be lifted up into the light again. You fear you will never leave the gloom behind and enter into a life of joy. People commonly feel this way when they have sinned egregiously and are depressed at how it has drastically changed their life for the worse. For example, people who have caused a lot of strife, abused their spouses, and then find themselves alienated from their families for a long time can feel this way. They feel that by their contentious behavior they've ruined their lives and have nothing but sorrow to look forward to. It is good to own sin, but thinking this way contains a subtle problem. It assumes that joy can return only when the consequences of sin are gone, and that is not true. In fact, when our circumstances are hard and uninviting, we are being given an opportunity to find all of our joy in Christ. After all, we are not told to rejoice only when our circumstances are pleasing to us. True Christianity is noted for giving a basis for joy even when outwardly everything appears to be going wrong. If the consequences of your sin gall you every day, take it as God leading you to stop idolizing things on the earth. Take it as God giving you an opportunity to put Him, His Word, and His Christ at the center of your life. Realize that God wants you to "rejoice in the Lord always" (Phil. 4:4). Repent of your worldliness and get your soul into a state in which your joy is based on biblical truth, not whether your circumstances are pleasant. If you do so, you'll be the sort of person who can provide stability to a family rather than adding more strife and turmoil. "In the fear of the LORD there is strong confidence, and His children will have a place of refuge" (Prov. 14:26).

In this chapter, we have looked at James's final two observations on how to come to God humbly for the grace to help in our fight against sin. Over the past two chapters we described seven observations in all: we must submit to God, resist the devil, draw near to God, cleanse our hands, purify our hearts, be afflicted, and exchange laughter for mourning. When we come this way, God will lift us up. This is a wonderfully helpful picture of genuine repentance! It should provide food for thought if you profess Christ yet cannot depart from iniquity and causing strife. Test yourself by these Spirit-inspired qualities of true repentance. Perhaps you need to fall on your face before God in sorrow and true loathing of your sin.

But you may be someone who quails in fear at this exposition of genuine repentance, wondering if you'll ever be able to repent well enough. James doesn't mean to imply that you must repent perfectly before you can have assurance. You must realize that God accepts imperfect faith as long as it's sincere. Remember the man we mentioned earlier who wanted Jesus to heal his son and said to Him "I believe; help my unbelief!" (Mark 9:24). Jesus didn't tell the man to go away until he could drum up better faith. He healed the man's son when he demonstrated sincere though imperfect faith. He will respond to any and all who come to Him this way. It's true of repentance too; it has to be, for you've never done anything perfectly. Cast yourself down before the Lord and tell Him even your repentance isn't good enough. Say "I repent; help my unrepentance." Casting yourself completely on Him in despair of self is the heart of coming to God rightly. But you don't need to accept your current quality of repentance either. God can give greater degrees of real submission to God, real drawing near to Him, and real sorrow for sin. David asked God to give him a clean heart (Ps. 51:10), which shows that he relied on God's transformative power even for his own godly thoughts and feelings. Without God you can do nothing, not even repent well, and all true dealings with God involve lifting up empty hands to Him, asking Him to fill them. When you see deficiency in yourself, even in your repentance, you have an opportunity to seek His all-sufficiency. He makes up for your lack. There is an element of mystery to it, but you must trust Him for grace to help you seek Him for grace, and then never stop seeking Him. If you do seek Him for grace, and if you do experience His empowerment against sin (to some degree at least), rejoice greatly, for these things are evidence of God's merciful working in your soul.

Study Questions

1. According to John Bunyan, what is presumption?

2. Why is sorrow a necessary aspect of repentance?

3. Why is it a mistake to attempt to judge how much sorrow is enough sorrow to be saved?

4. How would you counsel a person who says, "I realized that when I repented I had some false motives; I think my whole salvation is a sham!"

5. Does true sorrow affect one's demeanor?

6. Does genuine repentance and sorrow over sin lead to a dour life of no joy? Why or why not?

7. Why do people fail to gain power over sin in their lives? List some reasons found in the chapter.

8. How does Ralph Venning expose the terrible sinfulness of sin?

9. Why is it important to live *coram Deo*?

10. How might a person mistake the promise "Humble yourself and God will lift you up"?

11. Explain how miserable circumstances, even ones caused by your sin, are an opportunity.

CHAPTER 6

The Pride of Subtly Judging God

Do not speak evil of one another, brethren. He who speaks evil of a brother and judges his brother, speaks evil of the law and judges the law. But if you judge the law, you are not a doer of the law but a judge. There is one Lawgiver, who is able to save and to destroy. Who are you to judge another?
—JAMES 4:11–12

At this point James might appear to be shifting gears, but he still has human pride in mind as well as verbal mistreatment of others; he still is connected to the previous discussion about strife in relationships. James explores how pride manifests itself so that we can identify its subtle ways. He wants us to sense its implications easily so we will vigorously oppose it with conviction and eradicate it by God's grace. This time, pride shows itself not only in relational strife but in subtly judging God. James wants us to see how exalting oneself is a terrible sin and that it doesn't just manifest itself in contention, but in many ways.

James refers to the strife people are causing—speaking evil of others. *Speaking evil* is a phrase referring to abusive, derogatory, demeaning speech. A modern person might use the term *trash-talking*. James forbids this sort of speech, but his main purpose is to show how trash-talking against someone is actually an attack on God's authority. It is a power grab against Him. As such it is a stunning display of arrogance, but we often don't see it for what it is.

To help us see the implications of our abusive speech against others, James points out that by speaking evil of others, we speak evil of God's law. In every abusive word against another person, there is an abusive word against God. The act of trash-talking others is trash-talking God. That is what James says: "He who speaks evil of a brother and judges his brother, speaks evil of the law and judges the law." But someone might wonder how this is true. The abuse was directed at the person, not at God. How is trash-talking others automatically trash-talking God's law?

James helpfully answers this question: "If you judge the law, you are not a doer of the law but a judge." He's saying that people are not in a position of authority over the law, and they shouldn't think they are. We are not God; we are under Him and His kingly authority. We must obey His law, not set ourselves over it. The law forbids abusive speech; therefore, if you engage in it, you are by definition abusing the law that forbids it. To break God's law against trash-talking is to trash-talk the law.

Here is where the arrogance can be seen. By speaking evil of others, you have exalted yourself above God. You have essentially said, "Yes, I know You have commanded us to love one another. I know You've said to be filled with the Spirit—with love, peace, and gentleness. But I'm going to disregard You. I have decided that I know better. I have a good reason to speak evil." This is immense arrogance and a rejection of God's lordship. Jesus asked quite simply, "Why do you call Me 'Lord, Lord,' and not do the things which I say?" (Luke 6:46). Deciding to overturn the king's law is a direct challenge to His kingship. It is to set oneself up as a rival king. It is a usurpation, a coup, an attempt at a hostile take-over. Breaking a commandment may seem subtle to us, but to God it is most certainly not subtle. We find it so only because we are insensitive to God's rights and prerogatives.

In reality there is just one king and lawgiver. There is just one judge. He alone has power to eternally save or eternally destroy. He has the authority, not us, and if we challenge it, whose side are we choosing to be on? We are clearly choosing to be against God. What right do we have to challenge His authority? We have no right, yet we challenge it every time we sin.

It ought to be immensely humbling to realize that we have so often expressed rebellion against God and even rejected His lordship. It ought to bring us down to the dust in tears and remorse, dismayed at our behavior, even as we cry to God for mercy in Christ. We ought to recant our rebellion and restore fealty to our one and only king. And when we remember the marvelous news that Christ receives sinful, repentant people, we will come back to Him with the humility and joy that is always requisite in sinners who are saved by grace alone. But we also ought to come with greater zeal to oppose sin and with persistent prayer for strength to wage war against it.

Seeing the full implications of our acts of sin should cause us to live with an immense feeling of carefulness and even fear. Do you see how prone we are to revolt? We ought to see ourselves as people of oil-soaked tinder in a world full of sparks, sparks that so easily cause us to ignite and roar into flame. We ought to have a serious self-awakening as to our inherent weakness. In our fallen natures we are rebels, and we set ourselves up as rival lords against the Lord. The worst part is that we can do it without so much as a thought. There is something satanic about that, something infernal. James had said earlier that the tongue is "set on fire by hell" (James 3:6).

Seeing the full implications of our sin ought to cause us to exercise care over all aspects of our lives. We will distrust ourselves, particularly our knee-jerk, spontaneous reactions to things: "He sins who hastens with his feet" (Prov. 19:2). We will give careful thought to our speech, our answers and replies: "The heart of the righteous studies how to answer, but the mouth of the wicked pours forth evil" (Prov. 15:28). We will be "slow to speak, slow to wrath" (James 1:19). We will make decisions carefully, seeking the Lord's mind in all things. As Paul says, we will "walk circumspectly," which means carefully, like walking barefoot through broken glass (Eph. 5:15). Bunyan's allegory *Pilgrim's Progress* presents the Christian life as a narrow road to heaven full of dangers, toils, and snares along the way. Bunyan's sobering view of life is far more biblical than many today might suppose.

Seeing the full implications of our sin ought also to engender in us a zealous reliance on God. When we realize the poison we carry about in our flesh, we will begin to rely more and more on God's Spirit, whom the Father gave us to counteract the flesh (Gal. 5:16). We will seek continual filling by the Spirit, and we will seek God with renewed vigor for help against ourselves and for assistance in mortifying our flesh. We need His help not merely for our outward actions but for our hearts. "Set a guard, O LORD, over my mouth; keep watch over the door of my lips. Do not incline my heart to any evil thing" (Ps. 141:3–4). As John Owen said, "Always be killing sin or it will be killing you."[1]

---

1. Owen, *Mortification of Sin*, 5.

People do not rely on God's grace unless they feel the need for it. James here is showing us our need. We are dyed-in-the-wool rebels. We commit sin almost as easily as breathing. Even as Christians we continually fight and war against our flesh and find ourselves doing and saying things we regret. And James shows us here that each sin we commit is a great crime against the Lord and Judge of all. James has pulled the scales from our eyes so that we can see the gravity of one act of sin. We must take a long look at ourselves, as we really are, and then run to Christ as our only hope, remembering that He is abundantly able and willing to pardon.

James refers here to speaking evil of others, but sin is not merely a matter of our actions. Sin is committed in the heart as well as the actions, as can be seen by James's reference to the sin of judging, or hatefully condemning people. Elsewhere James speaks of hidden inward sin too; he speaks of inward sighing and grumbling against people. "Do not grumble against one another, brethren, lest you be condemned. Behold, the Judge is standing at the door!" (James 5:9). The word translated *grumble* refers to an inner expression of complaint. You might say an inward sigh or groan. James is showing how God's law has jurisdiction over our thoughts and feelings as well as our actions. A sin in the heart is still a sin, though it doesn't come out of its den. You may not be the sort of person to speak evil; you may be a more reserved individual with a personality that avoids conflict. But we all are sinners, and we all commit sin. Thus, we all need to realize that whether we are extroverts or introverts, we revolt against God and need to be cautious and God-dependent in our fight against sin, for God sees it all (Heb. 4:13).

As the Westminster Confession of Faith puts it, "Sanctification is throughout, in the whole man; yet imperfect in this life, there abiding still some remnants of corruption in every part; whence ariseth a continual and irreconcilable war, the flesh lusting against the Spirit, and the Spirit against the flesh...yet, through the continual supply of strength from the sanctifying Spirit of Christ, the regenerate part doth overcome; and so, the saints grow in grace" (13.2–3).

Study Questions

1. Explain how speaking evil of a person is automatically speaking evil of God's law.

2. Explain how a sin is an attempted hostile take-over against God.

3. Why is it hard for us to see how our sin reflects negatively on God?

4. James is interested in waking us up to the full implications of our sin. Once we become sensitized to those implications, what experiential results occur in our souls? List several from the chapter.

5. Imagine that you know people who think they would never cause strife or speak evil of anybody and that they therefore don't exalt themselves over God and subtly judge His law. How might you help them see their error?

CHAPTER 7

The Pride of a Self-Sufficient Spirit

Come now, you who say, "Today or tomorrow we will go to such and such a city, spend a year there, buy and sell, and make a profit"; whereas you do not know what will happen tomorrow. For what is your life? It is even a vapor that appears for a little time and then vanishes away. Instead you ought to say, "If the Lord wills, we shall live and do this or that."
—JAMES 4:13–15

James is intent on our seeing pride for the terrible evil that it is. So far he has told us that pride leads us to exalt our desires and to cause strife when they go unfulfilled (James 4:1–10). Causing strife is by nature a prideful insurrection against God's lordship as our lawgiver (4:11–12). Now, to finish off his chapter on a somber note, James explains how pride is an independent, self-sufficient attitude that actually is a form of atheism.

James Confronts Us Again

James says, "Come now, you who say…." This is a way of confronting us again and pointing out another deep problem we need to consider. We've got a serious spiritual issue to address in our lives—how we think, talk, and act about the future, particularly our plans for it. Our attitude about the future shows how we think about ourselves and how we think about God. We cannot worship God rightly until we think rightly.

James points out that if we blithely say we're going to travel somewhere and stay there for a time, carrying on a business and ending up with a profit, this speaks of the future as if it were totally in our control, and it leaves God out or diminishes His importance. It reflects a prideful and false view of humanity as well as a degraded and false view of God. Man cannot be right with God until he sees himself as small and sinful before Him, yet our default mode is to exalt ourselves and minimize Him. As Calvin said, "Man is never sufficiently touched and affected by the awareness of his lowly state until he has compared himself with God's majesty."[1] And we want to compare ourselves favorably to God!

Our descriptions of our plans—words that seem innocent to us—actually reflect a terrible and soul-destroying practical atheism that views God as though He were unrelated to circumstances. And such descriptions view ourselves as more relevant to our futures than God. Speaking of our future without reference to God and His sovereign control over it is to rebel against what is true about Him. It is to kick against objective reality. The fact is that God is far more relevant to what will happen than we are. "A man's heart plans his way, but the LORD directs his steps" (Prov. 16:9). We must see how easy it is to subtly reject a theocentric view of the world, to degrade the living God and attempt to remove Him from the considerations of life.

---

1. Calvin, *Institutes*, 1.1.3.

Therefore, James is once again showing us that ungodly pride, which ruins relationships with strife and contention, can pop up in ways that surprise us and seem subtle. James wants to sensitize us to pride and its many manifestations because it is an insidious and destructive evil, and we can so easily fall into it without even knowing it. It not only destroys relationships but also defies God. It exalts finite man and degrades the infinite God.

Pride Exalts Finite Man

James specifies two ways pride exalts finite man. Prideful thoughts tend to ignore the fact that man is ignorant of the future, and it ignores the reality of the brevity of life. People are actually stuck in a time line that doesn't allow for fast-forwarding or pausing. And that time line outlasts our short journey on it. Thus, we are ignorant and short-lived, yet we have the audacity to speak arrogantly about our plans.

We truly are ignorant of the future. I can't tell you how many times I've seen a character in a film say absurd things about the future. "Don't worry, it'll be OK," someone says to a person who has just been shot. "Everything's going to be all right," someone says when the world is coming apart. Of course, these comments are circumscribed by the fact that the movie's script is written in stone, so they are almost messages of comfort to the anxious viewer who is wondering how the movie will turn out. But taken as simple statements, they are obviously examples of spectacular overreach. In short, they are arrogant presumptions. James is right; no one knows what the future will bring. Who is to say that our end might come in an hour, a day, or a month? No one knows the future. We can analyze past patterns and speculate, but no one really can be sure (see Luke 12:16–21).

Not only are we ignorant of the future, but we truly are ephemeral. I first came across the term *ephemera* in reference to books. The term literally means "here for a day," and so it has been applied to printed matter that was originally produced for quick consumption and then tossed into the garbage. Interestingly, these works, such as paperbacks and comic books, have become collector's items, and people spend a lot of money and effort trying to preserve them. It once dawned on me that people are like that. We're here for a day, and we try desperately to preserve our lives, but inevitably we succumb to the ravages of time. We're like an old paperback book moldering on some dark shelf until the spine splits and the pages fall out. But our fate is far more poignant than that of a book, for we are not just ephemera, we are "sentient ephemera." Unlike a book, we partake of consciousness. And therein is the horror of death. We love, we laugh, we play, we aspire, we dream, yet the unconscious stones last longer than we do. The illustration James uses is that of a vapor, or mist: "What is your life? It is even a vapor." He probably is thinking of the mist that hovers over the earth in the morning but vanishes by noon. That is humankind— a mist that evaporates. We don't last.

James is saying we are ignorant and short-lived, and thus to speak about our future without reference to God, as if everything depends on our choices, is completely foolish. It wrongly exalts finite humans and ignores mankind's true condition. "A man's steps are of the LORD; how then can a man understand his own way?" (Prov. 20:24).

Pride Dishonors the Infinite God

The pride James is talking about not only wrongly exalts finite man but also degrades God. James says our futures depend on God's will first and foremost. "Instead you ought to say, 'If the Lord wills, we shall live and do this or that'" (James 4:15). Our futures do not depend on our choices but on God's choices! This puts God's sovereign will and providential control in its proper place in our thinking. He is utterly sovereign, so sovereign that He is far more in control of our futures than we are. If we go somewhere and find success, it is because God willed it.

God's sovereignty means that He is completely in control. Nearly all Christians believe in some form of sovereignty, but some people view God's control as extensive, or broad, only. He provides the outlines of things, they say, sustaining the world yet leaving an area in which man operates free from any divine constraint. God ensures the boat will get to the harbor to which He pointed it, but people are free to do as they will on board during the voyage. This raises a question—Is God sovereignly in control of only the big things but not the little things? Has God limited His control somewhat to make room for others to have control?

It is important to recognize that God's sovereignty is both extensive and intensive. He is in control of all the big things and each of the little things. James 4 shows both. He says to all who read, "You ought to say, 'If the Lord wills.'" The doctrine he's teaching applies to anyone who reads the words, including us! That's extensive control. God is the determining factor over all our futures. But the same statement also shows that sovereignty is intensive, for this doesn't just apply to all in some broad way, but it applies to every individual person. If it applies to "all," then it applies to "every." That means you. It means me. God's will determines my future and your future.

A similar text supports a view of sovereignty that is extensive and intensive. God "has made from one blood every nation of men to dwell on all the face of the earth, and has determined their preappointed times and the boundaries of their dwellings" (Acts 17:26). This text shows the broad extent of sovereignty. God determines when "every nation" comes to exist, how long it will last, and where it will dwell; that is, God decides the appointed times and boundaries of all nations. He decided when Rome would arise, how far its empire would reach, and when it would decline and go off the scene. It is the same with all other countries, kingdoms, and people groups. That is massive, extensive sovereignty! But what about individuals? How does this text show intensive sovereignty? Well, think of it this way. To decide when and where a nation would exist is to necessarily be in control of every person's decisions in making up the nation. Think of all the individuals who made decisions that led them to be part of the founding of the United States in 1776. God determined the times of all nations, and therefore He was sovereign not only over the United States but over every individual that was part of its inception as well as every individual that makes up its "boundaries" throughout the nation's existence. To be in control of the inception and boundaries of a nation is to be in control of the multitude of people and choices that determine them. God's sovereignty is massively extensive and intensely individual.

Many Bible texts show both the intensive and extensive nature of God's sovereignty. God sovereignly controls the details: "The lot is cast into the lap, but its every decision is from the LORD" (Prov. 16:33). He controls all the details that make up the whole. God "works all things according to the counsel of His will" (Eph. 1:11). The control God exercises is total—He guarantees all believers that everything works together for their good (Rom. 8:28), which is a promise that presupposes total control. He couldn't guarantee something so vast if He didn't exercise His will to ensure it. He couldn't guarantee it if there were other wills that determined whether it would be so. His will is *the* decisive factor. If He decides a thing will be, His will is conclusive. It will be. Therefore, God's control is extensive, intensive, and total. That's sovereignty.

But James is adding one more thing to the picture of God's sovereignty. He is saying that God is sovereign not merely over the present but over the future as well. We should say, "If God wills, we will go and do this or that." God doesn't just know the future; His will controls it. "My counsel shall stand, and I will do all My pleasure" (Isa. 46:10). God's will determines a person's future, not the person's will: "There are many plans in a man's heart, nevertheless the LORD's counsel—that will stand" (Prov. 19:21). God's will is determinative, and this is the way it always will be. "The counsel of the LORD stands forever, the plans of His heart to all generations" (Ps. 33:11). Can you see how these verses show God's sovereign control over the future? James's words coincide with the testimony of Scripture as a whole.

To sum up, God's control is extensive, intensive, and total over the past, present, and future. He is God Almighty, the Alpha and Omega. He is the Lord of all, and He always will be.

Some people feel that to accept such a strong view of God's sovereignty removes people's responsibility. There is a tendency in people to swing to extremes like a pendulum. "OK, if I'm not in control, then that means I'll just sit and do nothing." But this isn't a biblical response at all. The Bible upholds a very strong view of God's sovereignty, as we have seen, but it also teaches that people are responsible for their actions. "Each of us shall give account of himself to God" (Rom. 14:12). We all have a will, and we act according to our nature. Fallen people act according to their fallen natures, and believers in Christ, who have the Holy Spirit, are enabled graciously by Christ to act according to their new natures (Rom. 6:18–22). Therefore, God is totally sovereign, but man acts according to his own will and is responsible for his actions. It is important to note, however, that God's will is sovereign, or overruling; that is, man's will should not be understood to overrule it or be equal to it. God has decreed all things (Eph. 1:11), and "no one can restrain His hand" (Dan. 4:35). "There is no wisdom or understanding or counsel against the LORD" (Prov. 21:30).

Now that we've considered the strong view of God's sovereignty that James teaches, let's home in on his main point—if we speak of the future as if it were unrelated to God's will, we deny the Lord who controls it. We speak as if He didn't exist. It's subtle atheism. Human pride wants to remove God from consideration, but James is saying that God is near and involved in everything, and He is in control of it all.

This same prideful exalting of ourselves and diminishing of God causes strife. We fight because we are looking at the circumstances, not at God. We remove Him from consideration. Seeing Him as sovereign is key in healing strife in our lives because it is disregarding and diminishing Him that causes us to exalt our desires and seek to improve our lot with wrong words and actions. Treating God as sovereign will cause us to seek Him rather than ourselves and our own devices. Seeing Him as sovereign and acting on that truth by trusting and seeking Him will keep us from acting independently and resorting to sinful anger and abuse.

The right response to God's sovereignty is not to relieve ourselves of responsibility, feel that there is no use in trying, or fear that God is a big ogre. These are common misconstruals of the doctrine of God's sovereignty. Rather, James exhorts us to think of God's will as the determining factor in our lives and then talk that way. "Lord willing, I'll move there and start that business and make a profit." Of course, prayer is also a correct response to God's sovereignty. Since God's will is the determining factor over what happens, seek God for every blessing you want out of life. Include Him in every thought and decision. See Him as the determining factor in everything—big, little, future, possible, or certain. When you do not get what you hope to attain, seek the sovereign Lord rather than fall into agitation, fear, and strife. To do anything less is to fail to grasp who God really is—our sovereign Lord who gives grace to help in time of need: "God, from all eternity, did, by the most wise and holy counsel of his own will, freely, and unchangeably ordain whatsoever comes to pass: yet so, as thereby neither is God the author of sin, nor is violence offered to the will of the creatures; nor is the liberty or contingency of second causes taken away, but rather established" (WCF 3.1).

Sometimes it is easy to feel that if God is more relevant to our future happiness than we are, then the future is fearful and scary. I've seen this firsthand; when some people see the doctrine of God's sovereignty, they become less confident and peaceful rather than more so. But this shows us how committed we are to our own sense of control. We literally feel more at peace thinking we are in control than thinking God is. How offensive that must be to God! This is what James is trying to get us to feel: that our sin is an offense and an insult to the sovereign Lord who deserves our trust, not our skepticism. We must repent of our distrust and must rejoice that God receives sinful people and helps His weak and tottering lambs.

God wants the truth about Him to affect our emotional state. He wants us to believe in who He is and be comforted. When the disciples were in the boat with Christ on the Sea of Galilee, there was a storm that threatened to submerge the boat. Jesus was asleep, but the disciples were terrified and awakened Him, asking Him the reproachful question, "Do You not care that we are perishing?" Jesus awakened, stilled the storm with a simple word, and then asked a penetrating question: "Why are you so fearful?" (Mark 4:38–40). Jesus was saying that their faith in Him should have affected their emotional state. It should have cast out fear. He basically told them that their faith was so small it was next to nothing (see Matt. 8:26; Mark 4:40). Perhaps the reason why we have no peace is that we are not grasping the truth about God in faith. Perhaps our souls are empty of knowledge about God. We haven't stocked them with truth. Jesus is telling us that people who truly believe have their emotions affected by their faith. It could be said that peace and joy are an acid test of whether our faith is real.

Does God's sovereignty breathe comfort into your soul? Do you delight to know that God controls all things and has ordained whatever comes to pass? Does that fact make you breathe easier? Does it calm your agitated thoughts and make life more bearable? If it doesn't, perhaps it is because you subtly blame God for sin—sin that perhaps has harmed your life or the life of someone you love. When distrusting thoughts about God enter our minds, it is important to remember Jesus Christ entered our world of His own free will and suffered in it far more than we ever will. He made Himself vulnerable to the world's hatred, its harm, its scorn. God is not aloof or untouchable, decreeing sins gleefully as He sits far away. He hates sin but loves sinners, and He will stop at nothing to save His children even from their own evil. God is not to blame for sin—people are. If we accept this, we can realize that the God who ordained that people would sin also decreed that Christ would redeem sinners by shedding His own blood. The love of God is declared to us by Christ's death (Rom. 5:8).

Admit your own sin and guilt before God, and God's love and grace will stun you once more; you will be able to take comfort that this God who loves you so is at the helm of the universe. You may not understand how God's sovereignty and human responsibility totally mesh, but you'll know you can trust such a loving God despite your not fully understanding. The sovereign hand that rules the universe is nail-scarred.

Once you have humbly reaffirmed your faith in God's essential goodness and benevolence based on His grace in Christ, thinking on God's attributes will refresh and invigorate you, not frighten you. God's omniscience—the fact that He knows all—will not be a threat but will assure you that He can't learn anything about you that will surprise Him and cause Him to shrink back from you. It will assure you that He cannot be taken by surprise by circumstances and thus fail to carry out His plan to save His children (Ps. 147:5). God's omnipotence—the fact that He has all power—will not make you feel intimidated, but you will delight that the God who saved your soul is completely able to protect you just as He promises (Ps. 23:6). God's eternality—the fact that He transcends time—will thrill you because you will see that God's ways never become obsolete, and you can depend on Him to remain the same, unchangeable from eternity to eternity (Ps. 90:1–2; Mal. 3:6).

Charles Spurgeon said it best: "There is, in contemplating Christ, a balm for every wound.... Would you lose your sorrows? Would you drown your cares? Then go plunge yourself in the Godhead's deepest sea; be lost in his immensity; and you shall come forth as from a couch of rest, refreshed and invigorated. I know nothing which can so comfort the soul, so calm the swelling billows of grief and sorrow; so speak peace to the winds of trial, as a devout musing upon the subject of the Godhead."[2]

Study Questions

1. Explain how our words about our future plans reflect our faith or our lack of faith.

2. How does prideful speech about the future relate to causing strife?

3. How does sinful speech about the future wrongfully exalt finite man?

---

2. Charles Spurgeon, *The New Park Street Pulpit* (1855; repr., Pasadena, Tex.: Pilgrim Publications, 1990), 1:1.

4. Explain the term *sentient ephemera*. What is its relevance to the discussion?

5. How does sinful speech about the future degrade God?

6. What does it mean that God's sovereignty is both extensive and intensive? How do we know God's sovereignty is both?

7. What verses teach that God's sovereign control is total?

8. Is God sovereign over the future? How do we know?

9. Explain how a person's causing strife is related to unbelief in God's sovereignty. Why is seeing God as sovereign a key to healing strife?

10. What are some common misconstruals of God's sovereignty?

11. When tempted to distrust God, why is it important to remember Jesus Christ?

⌐

Our Responsibility to Do
Right by God's Grace

*But now you boast in your arrogance. All such boasting is
evil. Therefore, to him who knows to do good and does not
do it, to him it is sin.*
—JAMES 4:16–17

Chapter 4 of James concludes on a sobering note. He essentially tells us that our prideful boastings are evil, and he holds us responsible to do right by God's grace.

Evil Boastings

James says that when we express confidence in our pride, we are in sin. He is talking about self-confidence. Who else is there to put confidence in if you will not trust the Lord? If you will not trust God, you will put your faith in humanity in some way—either yourself or other people. This sort of humanistic self-confidence is evil because it dishonors God. It is this tendency to exalt in and trust self that leads to dishonoring God in our plans (James 4:13–15), speaking evil of Him and His law (4:11–12), and causing strife with each other (4:1–10).

The world is full of people who make money telling people to trust in themselves. Self-help gurus are always encouraging people to unlock the potential within them, to realize that they are the keys to their own happiness, and to use the unlimited power of positive thinking and its potential for change and progress. The problem with nearly all of these sorts of popular thinkers is that they promote a self-defined change, carried out through the power of self, for the sake of self. In other words, you ask, "What do I truly want?" and make that your goal. Then you discipline yourself to achieve it through constant and various techniques of the mind and the will. All along the way you do these things because "you are worth the effort, and you deserve a better life." It is seeking what you want, for yourself, and through your own power. It is individualism.

Having heard self-help speakers on several occasions, and having had friends who listened closely to them and then repeated to me what they heard, it occurred to me that what these speakers teach is Christless sanctification. Christians in ancient times would no doubt say that it is a variation on an ancient heresy called Pelagianism. Pelagius taught that people are born without a sin nature and can choose to love and please God all on their own without need for divine assistance. But the Bible teaches quite the opposite (e.g., John 6:44). And it is quite clear that godly change is defined by God, carried out through Christ's empowerment, and accomplished for God's glory (John 15:5; 1 Cor. 10:31). Individualism seeks what I want, for myself, and through my own power. A Christian seeks what God wants, for God, and through God's power.

Our culture is filled with individualist power fantasies. It is rife with stories about people who find it within them to accomplish something great through the power of human might. In the past decade, superhero stories have dominated the film industry, stories about muscle-bound people smacking down bad guys and overcoming threats and problems. These stories ultimately serve the purpose of wish fulfillment. People wish they could smack down their problems and make a better world by quick thinking and a powerful fist, so they enjoy watching fantasies about others doing so in dramatic fashion.

People who are in trying circumstances often fantasize about the things they wish they could do or say. They dream about telling off their boss, running away from home, helping someone they love get better, saying what they really think, or even committing physical violence against someone they hate. It's when these urges manifest themselves in life that strife and contention can come about. In circumstances in which there is some sort of misery, you will be tested as to whether you will solve your problems through "the arm of the flesh" or through God. The "arm of the flesh" is a biblical expression that occurs in Jeremiah 17: "Thus says the LORD: 'Cursed is the man who trusts in man and makes flesh his strength, whose heart departs from the LORD.... Blessed *is* the man who trusts in the LORD, and whose hope is the LORD" (Jer. 17:5, 7).

When Israel faced trouble, they were famous for depending on the help of people and other nations, not God (Isa. 31:3). The "arm" was a metaphor for strength or help (Ex. 6:6; Ps. 89:21). We turn either to people or to God for help. Those are the only two options. Calling the help of people an "arm of flesh" is a way to point out its weakness. "All flesh is grass" (Isa. 40:6). Grass bends and withers, and flesh is like it; it is inherently weak and short-lived. To depend on the help and wisdom of humankind, even of yourself, is foolish. "Lean not on your own understanding" (Prov. 3:5). Individualism makes no sense.

It is God who is everlasting and all-wise. Listen to Him, depend on Him, call to Him for aid, trust Him for the future.

People who cause strife are depending on the arm of the flesh. Their hope, or expectation, is wrapped up in self-confidence. They are placing confidence in their own way of solving their problems and not submitting to God's ways. This wrong self-reliance is what James means when he says that they boast in their arrogance. We must renounce self-reliance and rely on God for grace and strength in order to deal with difficult situations in a way that doesn't cause strife.

Individualism might be considered a good thing if it means taking responsibility for one's actions and seeking to use one's time and resources in a right way, regardless of others' bad examples. When someone finally says, "I'm sick of my problems, and I'm going to do something about them, no matter what," it's a good thing. But people are wrong when they rely on self as the means to accomplish things as if God didn't exist or as if He weren't the One with whom we have to do (Heb. 4:13). People are also wrong when they think they are sufficient to deal with hardships and to change and grow spiritually. We must seek all things from God's hand. A good sort of individualism says, "I must take responsibility, but I must go forward on my knees. God alone is all-sufficient, not me, so I will set my face like flint to seek Him for everything, including help with my sin and strife."

Our Responsibility to Do Right

James has opened for us many fresh avenues of thought. He has shown us how our pride and unbelief exalt our desires to the degree that we create strife because of them. He has shown us how to repent and resolve the conflict we cause, and he has added some additional help showing us how pride is a disease that pervades our souls and manifests itself in subtle but God-dishonoring ways. It is a remarkably helpful chapter.

James finishes on a note of personal responsibility that is quite simple and intuitive. James essentially says to us, "There, now you have heard all this. You now know what is right, so you're in sin if you don't practice it." He says that God expects His people to do what is right. There is no room for a licentious religion that is slack about morality. Much modern Christianity is swamped in an error called antinomianism, which says that God's law is not important. Anyone who wants God's comforting promises but not God's commands has fallen into this error.

Years ago, a teenage girl who had been raised a Roman Catholic began attending the church I pastor, and she listened intently to the message of the gospel. She realized that what I was preaching from the Bible differed dramatically from what she'd heard as a child. But she wanted to be sure that what she was hearing really was in the Bible. My wife and I took her, step by step, through the first four chapters of Romans, and she saw that it was true—salvation is by faith alone in Christ alone and not by works. After a time of indecision, when she was concerned about what her family might think, she submitted to the teaching of the Bible, and she made a profession of faith in Christ.

A couple of weeks later, she asked me a question after a church service. She had a lot of Christian friends in our town who did not attend our church, and she had begun noticing that their lifestyle was unconcerned with biblical morality. They got drunk, used foul language, and were promiscuous. This girl's question was, "Who is right, the people who say to live how you want? Or you guys, who are trying very hard to live differently?" She was dealing with the fact that our church was the only Christian community she knew that wasn't openly antinomian. It was many years ago, but I'm pretty sure I just showed her Romans 6. She realized that salvation by grace did not imply a life free from right and wrong. Grace doesn't erase or negate God's commands; it provides empowerment to obey them through the Spirit (Titus 2:11–12; Gal. 5:16).

James says that if we know what is right, we're in sin if we don't practice it. Let's review the things James wants us to practice. In the interest of summing up James 4, here is a handy list. It is not a list of dos and don'ts to check off like a grocery list. Think of it as what the Spirit is up to in your life. Think of this list as filled with Christ's goals for you, goals that He is currently at work fulfilling in you. Think of it as God's teaching for you to embrace and to seek Him about in prayer. Think of it as what you resolve to do by His grace and for His glory, depending on your union with Christ by faith in the gospel every step of the way.

1. Recognize that we sinfully exalt our desires over God when we cause strife.

2. Understand that we are so wicked that we can even turn prayer into a selfish exercise—primarily about us and our wants and personal satisfaction. Our religion can be the worship of ourselves under the guise of worshiping God.

3. Accept the label of spiritual adulterer, and allow it to drive you to Christ in repentance.

4. Believe that God gives grace to the humble. Feel the need for that grace.

5. Come to God humbly to receive grace to help in your battle against sin.

6. Come to God humbly by resisting the devil, coming back and drawing near to God, cleansing both heart and hands. Be in genuine sorrow over your terrible sin.

7. Recognize that sinning against a person is sinning against God.

8. Recognize that dismissing or breaking a command is setting oneself up as a judge over God's law. See this as the act of defiance that it is.

9. Understand that speaking of your future decisions without referring to God, who is the truly relevant one, is a subtle form of atheism. See how easily pride works its way into the heart and affects everything in a subtle way.

10. Think of your life and future as completely in God's hands and speak accordingly.

11. Avoid self-reliance. An independent, self-sufficient spirit is dishonoring to the sovereign Lord as well as a denial of our weak and transitory selves.

Afterword

In Colossians 2:6–7 the apostle Paul tells us that we are to be rooted in Christ and built up in Him. Our initial Christian experience is one of being rooted in Him. Our continued Christian experience is one of being built up in Him—that is, edified in keeping with that initial experience. Paul uses a horticultural metaphor (rooted) and a construction metaphor (built up) to demonstrate that our justification and our sanctification are connected to Christ.

Justification and sanctification are not the same thing, and there are grave consequences when people equate them. But they are of a piece in this sense: they both are all about relationship to Christ. In this book, James 4 has been shown to follow a pattern that feels almost evangelistic. You see your sin, become convicted, and flee to grace in Christ. To read James 4 and understand it might make you feel that you are being asked to get saved all over again. You are being told that you need to see and really feel how you are making a mess of your life, how it is your fault, and how it all stems from your idolatry and abuse of God Himself. You need to accept that you are a sinner, a spiritual adulterer. You need to flee to grace in Christ, trusting God as a forgiving Father. And you need to decisively repent with true sorrow for sin. That all seems very evangelistic, and it is!

But it is simply reflecting what Paul says: there is a kinship between our continued Christian experience and our initial one. To put it most simply, as we continue on with the Lord, we keep running to Christ just as we did when we first came to Him. We are not losing our salvation and getting saved all over again. We are simply fleeing to Christ over and over for help in our daily struggle against sin. That continual fleeing to Christ is a repetition of our very first flight to Him. Our roots are in Him, and our continued building up is firmly connected to Him too.

This is actually quite wondrous! People often feel that their Christian experience has dried up. Their feelings have changed. They think, "I guess I shouldn't expect that the joy of my salvation would last forever. Maybe I'm just older, and excitement about Christ is a thing of my youth." Rubbish! Since when did rejoicing in the Lord become a thing to be laid aside like a relic of our younger years? The secret to always rejoicing in the Lord is feeling that there is a reason to do so, and nothing will do that more than feeling like a sinner yet knowing beyond a shadow of a doubt that Christ's grace conquers all, and all your sin was nailed to the cross, where it was blotted out forever. Even more, God provides power over sin now through the Spirit of Christ.

James's discussion is based on a presupposition—we should expect God's power for victory over sin. This may sound self-evident, but it is actually quite a revolutionary thought. Think of what happens when one no longer believes in the possibility of power over sin, when one denies that this power is available, or when one has failed so many times one thinks it's hopeless. When such thoughts sink into your mind like a terrible spiritual poison, you do not expect substantial spiritual victory in the Christian life, you lower your standards, you excuse your sins, and your life becomes one of presuming on grace. You expect God to save you without sanctifying you.

An approach to the Christian life that tolerates sin accepts the reality of grace for forgiveness but denies its existence for sanctification. It doesn't expect much from God, and thus it denies the Scripture's very clear testimony that when God saves a person, He always transforms that person's life. We have warrant in Scripture to expect substantial victory over sin, though not perfect victory in this life, and we have no victory at all without spiritual struggle (Rom. 8:13). Have you dishonored God by tolerating sin, disbelieving His promise of sanctifying grace, and stifling your conscience with vain hopes of forgiveness without holiness? Turn to the promises of the gospel now, depending on the filling of the Holy Spirit and committing to living a life that is pleasing to God by His grace and for His glory.

It is apparent to me that a chapter such as James 4 is one of the most important correctives for our particular era. Our times are corrupt and debased in the extreme. They are times in which people expect very little holiness and experience very much strife, contention, and every form of evil. Many peoples' lives have become so deluged by evil that some professing Christians have forsaken the idea that life could be any different. James 4 tells us that it can and ought to be different, that we should insist that it be different. More importantly, God has graciously given us union with Christ and the presence of His Holy Spirit to empower us to be different. We must seek the Lord to gain the grace He gives to the humble, grace for help against ourselves and our sinful habits. Our era is marked by pride as well as unbelief and covetousness. But rather than wading any further into the cesspool, we should look to the golden promises of grace once more. We should believe them, fasten our hopes on them, make them our mindset, sing songs of praise because of them, and strive by God's grace to live up to them every day.

Memory Verses for Those Who Would Oppose Strife

When tempted to commit sin, we must draw from the Word of God stored up in a Spirit-filled heart (Ps. 119:11; Gal. 5:16). But storing up is not enough. Christ set the example of using specific statements of Scripture to counter specific temptations, very much like wielding a sword in battle (Matt. 4:1–11; Eph. 6:17). You must be familiar with specific statements in the Bible that address particular temptations so you can use them to resist the devil's advances. Below are some select Bible verses that will help in mortifying the sin of strife. Some of them condemn that particular sin or promote its opposite; others offer hope in the character of God and the promise of His gospel; still others help us frame our prayers in gospel terms. When taken together, they all provide a battery of spiritual resources for a believer's fight of faith.

- By pride comes nothing but strife. (Prov. 13:10)

- Where do wars and fights come from among you? Do they not come from your desires for pleasure that war in your members? (James 4:1)

- There is one who speaks like the piercings of a sword, but the tongue of the wise promotes health. (Prov. 12:18)

- The heart of the righteous studies how to answer, but the mouth of the wicked pours forth evil. (Prov. 15:28)

- The discretion of a man makes him slow to anger, and his glory is to overlook a transgression. (Prov. 19:11)

- Blessed are the peacemakers, for they shall be called sons of God. (Matt. 5:9)

- Let every man be swift to hear, slow to speak, slow to wrath. (James 1:19)

- The wisdom that is from above is first pure, then peaceable, gentle, willing to yield, full of mercy and good fruits, without partiality and without hypocrisy. Now the fruit of righteousness is sown in peace by those who make peace. (James 3:17–18)

- The fruit of the Spirit is love, joy, peace, longsuffering, kindness, goodness, faithfulness, gentleness, self-control. Against such there is no law. (Gal. 5:22–23)

- Remind them…to speak evil of no one, to be peaceable, gentle, showing all humility to all men. (Titus 3:1–2)

- A servant of the Lord must not quarrel but be gentle to all. (2 Tim. 2:24)

- If I regard iniquity in my heart, the Lord will not hear. (Ps. 66:18)

- Lament and mourn and weep! Let your laughter be turned to mourning and your joy to gloom. (James 4:9)

- We also, since the day we heard it, do not cease to pray for you, and to ask that you may be…strengthened with all might, according to His glorious power, for all patience and longsuffering with joy. (Col. 1:9, 11)

- Create in me a clean heart, O God, and renew a steadfast spirit within me. (Ps. 51:10)

- Set a guard, O LORD, over my mouth; keep watch over the door of my lips. (Ps. 141:3)

- For sin shall not have dominion over you, for you are not under law but under grace. (Rom. 6:14)

- He gives more grace. Therefore He says: "God resists the proud, but gives grace to the humble." (James 4:6)

- I will not let You go unless You bless me! (Gen. 32:26)

- For it is God who works in you both to will and to do for His good pleasure. (Phil. 2:13)

- Therefore, whether you eat or drink, or whatever you do, do all to the glory of God (1 Cor. 10:31)

- If you love Me, keep My commandments. (John 14:15)

- Humble yourselves in the sight of the Lord, and He will lift you up. (James 4:10)

- We know that all things work together for good to those who love God, to those who are the called according to His purpose. (Rom. 8:28)